English for Student Pharmacists 2

薬学生のための英語 2

In Accordance with the Revised Model Core Curriculum
for Pharmaceutical Education

Edited By
The Japan Association of Pharmaceutical English
(JAPE)

photographs by

iStockphoto

音声ファイルのダウンロード／ストリーミング

CDマーク表示がある箇所は、音声を弊社HPより無料でダウンロード／ストリーミングすることができます。トップページのバナーをクリックし、書籍検索してください。書籍詳細ページに音声ダウンロードアイコンがございますのでそちらから自習用音声としてご活用ください。

https://www.seibido.co.jp

English for Student Pharmacists 2

Copyright © 2019 by The Japan Association of Pharmaceutical English

All rights reserved for Japan
No part of this book may be reproduced in any form
without permission from Seibido Co., Ltd.

はじめに

　本書は、'薬剤師養成を目指す' 新制度の 6 年制薬学部で学ぶ 2、3 年生のための教科書です。日本薬学英語研究会 (JAPE) では、薬学を専攻する学生のための英語テキストに特化して、これまで、新たな薬学教育の柱である薬学教育モデル・コアカリキュラム（平成 14 年 8 月）の内容に即した「薬学英語 1、2」「薬学英語 1、2　改訂版」を刊行しました。また、授業で使用された先生方や学生のみなさんからのフィードバック、学会発表等における先生方からのコメントを参考に改訂を試みてきました。

　急激な社会の変化に伴い、「医療人である薬剤師」に求められる役割が益々多様になってきたため、平成 25 年 12 月に薬学教育モデル・コアカリキュラムの改訂が行われ、平成 27 年度より改訂コアカリによるカリキュラムが日本の薬学部・薬科大学で導入されています。この内容に即して、一昨年、新たに「薬学生のための英語 1」を刊行しました。

　今回、「薬学生のための英語 1」と同様に、テキスト編集に当たり、薬学分野で必要とされる英語に関する基本的事項を修得すること、専門性の高い語学能力を養うことを目的とし、改訂モデル・コアカリキュラムの内容 A 〜 G に沿った内容にすることを柱にしました。また、コアカリ改訂のポイントのひとつとして示された「薬剤師として求められる基本的な資質」（①薬剤師としての心構え、②患者・生活者本位の視点、③コミュニケーション能力、④チーム医療への参画、⑤基礎的な科学力、⑥薬物療法における実践的能力、⑦地域の保健・医療における実践的能力、⑧研究能力、⑨自己研鑽、⑩教育能力）を前提にして学修効果を期待できるものにすることを目指しました。

　コアカリの項目 A から G について、「浅くとも広く薬学分野に触れる」をモットーに以下のような章立てにしました。

A　基本事項から	Unit 1：信頼関係の構築【コミュニケーション】
	Unit 2：薬剤師の使命【患者安全と薬害の防止】
B　薬学と社会から	Unit 3：薬剤師と医薬品等に係る法規範
	【②医薬品等の品質、有効性及び安全性の確保に係る法規範】
C　薬学基礎から	Unit 4：C4 生体分子
	Unit 5：C6 生命現象の基礎
	Unit 6：C8 生体防御と微生物

D 衛生薬学から	Unit 7：D1 健康
	Unit 8：D2 環境
E 医療薬学 & F 薬学臨床	Unit 9：神経系の疾患と薬【精神神経疾患】
	Unit 10：免疫・炎症・アレルギーおよび骨・関節の疾患と薬 【免疫・アレルギー疾患】
	Unit 11：循環器系・血液系・造血系・泌尿器系・ 生殖器系の疾患と薬【高血圧症、心疾患、脳血管障害】
	Unit 12：呼吸器系・消化器系の疾患と薬
	Unit 13：代謝系・内分泌系の疾患と薬【糖尿病】
	Unit 14：感覚器・皮膚の疾患と薬
	Unit 15：病原微生物（感染症）・悪性新生物（がん）と薬
G 薬学研究	Unit 16：研究に必要な法規範と倫理

各章の構成は以下の通りです。

● READING

本文の長さは 550 語〜600 語程度、ほとんどがインターネットで容易に閲覧できる authentic（書換えていない、本文そのまま）の英文です。論理的にまとまった内容で極力読みやすい英文を厳選しています。傍注も充実していますから、果敢に取り組んでください。

● COMPREHENSION QUESTIONS

本文の後にさまざまな形式の内容確認問題があります。書かれている内容・知識・概念の把握に役立ててください。

● PHARMACEUTICAL TERMINOLOGY

薬学用語の基本が少しずつ学べるようになっています。巻末の Word Parts in Medical Terminology と合わせて効果的に語彙を増やしましょう。

● GRAMMAR

英文法は英語をさまざまに使用する時の強い味方です。薬学関連の文を用いて、文法の基本を復習するために確認問題を用意しました。巻末の文法一覧表も、是非、参考にしてください。

● LISTENING & SPEAKING

海外からのゲストを迎えて各国の薬学教育をテーマに日本の大学キャンパス内外で行われる会話や、薬局での患者と薬剤師による会話で構成されています。楽しんで取り組んでください。

● WRITING

薬理学を中心に、基本的な内容が英語で書けるように、練習問題を用意しました。専門用語にはヒントをつけました。日本文と英文の構造の違いを思い出しながら問題に取り組んでください。

コラム

「医療人である薬剤師」には、医療チームへの参加、多職種連携が求められています。今回は、薬学を専門とする大学の枠を超えて、同じ問題を扱う専門家の先生方にもさまざまな角度からコラムを執筆していただきました。留学経験談、病院の現場、在宅の現場からの声もしっかり受け止めて、今後に生かしてください。

　最後に、本書の刊行に当たり、深いご理解と全面的なご支援を賜りました株式会社成美堂代表取締役社長の佐野英一郎様と編集部の皆様に、心より感謝申し上げます。皆様の惜しみないご厚意を賜り、薬学部学生にとってより有益な教科書が完成しました。研究会一同、心よりお礼申し上げます。

日本薬学英語研究会一同

CONTENTS

はじめに iii

UNIT 1 Patient-Centered Communication in Pharmacy Practice
薬局業務における患者中心のコミュニケーション 1

剤形に関する表現 (1) / 8品詞 / 自己紹介 / ～することは不可欠だ /
ホスピス発祥の国でみえたもの

UNIT 2 Thalidomide: Tips for Entertainment Writers and Producers
サリドマイドを扱う脚本家と制作者への助言 8

剤形に関する表現 (2) / 名詞 / 日英の病院の比較 / ～を4つに分けられる /
ARTIST時々PHARMACIST

UNIT 3 FIP-WHO Technical Guidelines for Children-Specific
Preparations 小児用薬剤調製に関する共同ガイドライン 15

投薬・服薬に関する動詞 / 形容詞 / 国際薬学生連盟 / ～学は～を扱う /
非がん非ターミナルの小児の在宅医療

UNIT 4 Dioxins and Their Effects on Human Health
ダイオキシン類とヒトの健康への影響 22

調剤業務に関する動詞 / 動詞 / 講演会で質問 / ～に直面する /
前向きに考えることの大切さ

UNIT 5 Disorders of Amino Acid Metabolism アミノ酸代謝異常症 29

医薬用語に使われる接頭辞 (1) / 副詞 / 懇親会にて / ～を証明する /
国際交流から日本の麻酔管理の未来を目指して

UNIT 6 The Body's Second Line of Defence 体の第2防衛線 36

医薬用語に使われる接頭辞 (2) / 接続詞 / 薬学コアカリの英訳 / ～は～で決まる /
英語版薬学教育モデル・コアカリキュラム（平成25年度改訂版）公開

UNIT 7 Foodborne Germs and Illness 食物由来の病原菌と疾病 43

医薬品の投与経路に関する接頭辞 (1) / 前置詞 / オーストラリアの薬学教育 /
～は～に結合する / 英語の対応で安心を感じてもらおう

UNIT 8 Radiation Health Effects 放射線による健康への影響 50

医薬品の投与経路に関する接頭辞 (2) / 助動詞 / シンガポールの薬学教育 (1) /
～を変化させる / 世界に飛び込もう

UNIT 9 Parkinson's Disease パーキンソン病 57

一般用語と専門用語 / 関係代名詞 / シンガポールの薬学教育 (2) / ～作用はない /
製薬、医療機器企業における英語の必要性

UNIT 10 Rheumatoid Arthritis　　　関節リウマチ　　　64

処方箋の略語 (1) / 基本五文型 / 服薬指導 (1) / ～によって引き起こされる /
英語はBODY LANGUAGEでいい!?

UNIT 11 Heart Disease　　　心臓病　　　71

処方箋の略語 (2) / 無生物主語 / 問診票作成 / ～が有効である /
国際社会における薬剤師の役割

UNIT 12 What Is COPD　　　慢性閉塞性肺疾患　　　78

処方箋の略語 (3) / 仮定法 / 服薬指導 (2) / ～に使われる薬である /
真摯な対応ができる医療従事者には、教養と語学力が必須

UNIT 13 Diabetes　　　糖尿病　　　85

数量単位を表す表現 / 同格 / OTC薬販売 / ～に影響する / 在宅医療について

UNIT 14 Age-Related Macular Degeneration before and
after the Era of Anti-VEGF Drugs　　　加齢黄斑変性　　　92

さまざまな医薬品 (1) / 強調表現 / 服薬指導 (3) / ～として作用する /
専門職連携教育（IPE）について思うこと

UNIT 15 Antibiotic / Antimicrobial Resistance　　　抗菌薬耐性　　　99

さまざまな医薬品 (2) / 分詞構文 / 服薬指導 (4) / ～を～に保つ /
機械化による薬剤師業務の変革

UNIT 16 Academic Research in the 21st Century　　　21世紀の学術研究　　　107

さまざまな医薬品 (3) / 省略 / 副作用相談 / ～することを目指す /
医師国家試験には英語の問題がある!?

APPENDIX 1　文法一覧表　　　117

APPENDIX 2　Word Parts in Medical Terminology　　　121

APPENDIX 3　"PROFESSIONAL COMPETENCIES FOR PHARMACISTS"
「薬剤師として求められる基本的な資質」
薬学教育モデル・コアカリキュラム ―平成25年度改訂版―（英訳版・日本語版）　　　128

執筆者一覧　　　130

vii

Patient-Centered Communication in Pharmacy Practice

UNIT 1

個人間のコミュニケーションが患者中心の医療の基礎である。科学の飛躍的な発展により、現代の医療はきわめて高度で複雑なものになっている。

薬剤師と他の医療関係者との間だけでなく、薬剤師と患者の間での意思伝達が不明確であるならば、安全な薬物治療を促進することはできない。個人間のコミュニケーションは一見簡単に思えるが、その能力を高めることは生涯にわたって改善と訓練を要する複合的な過程であろう。

READING

 1-02

In order to meet their professional responsibilities, pharmacists have become more patient-centered in their provision of pharmaceutical care. Pharmacists have the potential to contribute even more to improved patient
5 care through efforts to reduce medication errors and improve the use of medications by patients. Using effective communication skills is essential in the provision of patient care.

Why is patient-centered communication so crucial to a
10 professional practice? Consider the following:

- A 36-year-old man was prescribed a fentanyl patch to treat pain resulting from a back injury. He was not informed that heat could make the patch unsafe to use. He fell asleep with a heating pad and died. The level of fentanyl in his
15 bloodstream was found to be 100 times the level it should have been (Fallik, 2006).

pharmaceutical care
薬学的ケア

medication error
投薬ミス

fentanyl
フェンタニル(鎮痛や麻酔に使われる強力な合成オピオイド)

patch 貼付剤

heating pad
温熱パッド(ベッドのシーツの下に敷く)

Normodyne
ノルモダイン（交感神経系の
α-アドレナリン受容体および
β-アドレナリン受容体を遮
断することで作用する抗高血
圧薬）
dispense 調剤する
Norpramin ノルプラミン
（うつ病の治療薬）
blurred vision
目のかすみ
tremor 震え

Cardizem CD
カルディゼムCD
（高血圧の治療薬。CDは
controlled delivery［放出制御］
の略）
sustained-release
徐放性
diltiazem ジルチアゼム
（カルディゼムの一般名）

immediate-release
即効型

checkup 検査

put A on B AにBを処方
する

et al.
〜ら（論文の著者が複数の場
合しばしば用いられる表記の
方法）
attribute A to B
AをBに帰する

adverse drug event
薬物有害事象
speculation 考察

dismiss 退ける

- A patient prescribed Normodyne for hypertension (HTN) was dispensed Norpramin. She experienced numerous side effects, including blurred vision and hand tremors. Since she knew that she was supposed to be taking the medication to treat HTN, even minimal communication between the pharmacist and patient about the therapy would have prevented this medication error (ISMP, 2004).

- An 83-year-old patient was given Cardizem CD (sustained-release diltiazem capsules) for blood pressure control. Because the capsule was too large to swallow, the patient chewed the medication. As a result, her pulse slowed twice to low levels, and the family contacted the pharmacist for advice. Upon learning that she was chewing the medication, the pharmacist suggested that the physician substitute immediate-release diltiazem tablets, which are easier to swallow. The prescription was changed and the patient did well for several months. Months later, the patient returned to her physician for a checkup. She was again put on Cardizem CD. She again began chewing the larger capsules. She became progressively weaker and died 3 weeks later (ISMP, 2010).

- A study by Weingart et al. (2005) found that, while 27% of patients experienced symptoms they attributed to a new prescription, many of these symptoms (31%) were not reported to the prescribing physician. The first author reported in a news release that "For every symptom that patients experienced but failed to report, one in five resulted in an adverse drug event that could have been prevented or made less severe." Authors' speculation on why patients failed to report symptoms focused on health care providers who do not inquire about problems with drug therapy and patients who dismiss the seriousness of side effects or do not want to be seen as complaining to physicians about treatments prescribed for them.

Pharmacists are accepting increased responsibility in assuring that patients avoid adverse effects of medications and reach desired outcomes from their therapies. The changing role of the pharmacist requires practitioners to switch from a "medication-centered" or "task-centered" practice to patient-centered care. As revealed in the situations described above, it is not enough for pharmacists and their staffs to simply provide medication in the most efficient and safest manner (i.e., focus on systems of drug order fulfillment). Pharmacists must participate in activities that enhance patient adherence and the wise use of medication (i.e., focus on patient-centered elements including patient understanding and actual medication-taking behaviors). Patient-centered care depends on your ability to develop trusting relationships with patients, to engage in an open exchange of information, to involve patients in the decision-making process regarding treatment, and to help patients reach therapeutic goals that are understood and endorsed by patients as well as by health care providers. Effective communication is central to meeting these patient care responsibilities in the practice of pharmacy.

Communication Skills in Pharmacy Practice, 6th edition, by Robert S. Beardsley, Carole L. Kimberlin, and William N. Tindall (2012) (Wolters Kluwer / Lippincott Williams & Wilkins) pp.1-2

References

Fallik D. *Drug patch safety triggers an FDA probe.* Philadelphia Inquirer, March 5, 2006. Retrieved May 5, 2006 from http://www.philly.com/mld/philly/living/health/14018264.htm

ISMP—Institute for Safe Medication Practice. *Medication Safety Alert.* 3(4), April 2004. Retrieved February 23, 2011 from http://www.ismp.org/Newsletters/ambulatory/Issues/community200404.pdf

ISMP—Institute for Safe Medication Practices. *Medication Safety Alert.* 2010. Retrieved February 23, 2011 from http://www.ismp.org/Newsletters/consumer/alerts/chewable.asp

Weingart SN, Gandhi TK, Seger AC, et al. Patient-reported medication symptoms in primary care. *Archives of Internal Medicine* 165:234-240, 2005.

1.1 COMPREHENSION QUESTIONS

Based on the passage, circle either T (true) or F (false) for each of the following statements.

1. In the case of a patient prescribed Normodyne, though the patient contacted the pharmacist to report her side effects, the pharmacist was unable to notice the medication error. (T / F)

2. In the case of an 83-year-old patient, if the patient had continued to take immediate-release diltiazem tablets after she returned to her physician for a checkup, she wouldn't have died so soon. (T / F)

3. In the study by Weingart et al. (2005), 27% of patients experienced symptoms which they thought were caused by a new prescription, but 31% of these symptoms were not known to the prescribing physician. (T / F)

4. According to Weingart, half of the symptoms that patients experienced but didn't report led to adverse drug events that could have been prevented. (T / F)

5. Pharmacists are responsible to their patients for the safety of medications and desired patient outcomes. (T / F)

1.2 PHARMACEUTICAL TERMINOLOGY

剤形に関する表現 (1)

　ここでは内用薬の剤形を挙げている。granuleとpowder、pillとtablet、syrupとliquidなど、似た剤形に注意しよう。

● 練習問題

Match each of the following words with its definition below and then translate the word into Japanese.

1. pill 　(　) _____　　4. lozenge (　) _____

2. capsule (　) _____　　5. syrup 　(　) _____

3. tablet 　(　) _____

(a) a small disc or cylinder of compressed solid medicine for swallowing whole

(b) a small round mass of solid medicine for swallowing whole

(c) a small soluble case of gelatin containing a dose of medicine, swallowed whole

(d) a small medicinal tablet, originally in the shape of diamond, taken for sore throats and dissolved in the mouth

(e) a thick, sweet liquid containing medicine

4

Unit 1　Patient-Centered Communication in Pharmacy Practice

1.3 GRAMMAR 「8品詞」

　英語では、伝統的に文の構成要素としての語を8種類の品詞に分けている。すなわち名詞、代名詞、形容詞、副詞、動詞、前置詞、接続詞、間投詞である。ただし、同じ語でも使い方が異なれば意味も働きも異なるので注意しよう。

練習問題

次の各文の下線部に注意して、全文を日本語に訳しなさい。

1. All electromagnetic radiation is made up of <u>minute</u> packets of energy or 'particles,' called photons.

2. Have a <u>hand</u> in your health decisions. Together with your health care professionals, agree on a medicine <u>treatment</u> plan that works for you.

3. Cutting-edge technology sheds <u>light</u> on antibiotic resistance.

4. Cohort studies in North America and Western Europe have reported an increased risk of mortality associated with long-term exposure to <u>fine</u> particles (PM$_{2.5}$).

5. We often take <u>water</u> quality for granted in daily life and in our work.

1.4 LISTENING & SPEAKING 1-03

Listen to the following conversation and fill in the blanks based on the Japanese.

In a seminar room.

Prof. Miller: Hello, everyone! Welcome to my seminar. This is a private one, so I'm afraid you will not receive credit. But I'm sure you will learn a lot and have a good time.

Shunsuke: 1. _____.
(先生のゼミはいつもおもしろいと思います)

Prof. Miller: Thank you, Shunsuke. Oh, by the way, he is a fifth-year student and has been attending this seminar for the past four years.

Marina: Wow. I am Marina and am a freshman. 2. _____
_____. Nice to meet you.
(私の夢は病院薬剤師になることです)

Masayuki: Hi, my name is Masayuki and I am in my third year. 3. _____
_____.
(去年、僕はミラー教授の通常の英語の授業に出席しました)
Thank you.

Yuria: Hello, I'm Yuria. I'm a fourth-year student from Okinawa. 4. _____
_____.
(去年からこのゼミのメンバーです)

Prof. Miller: Well, everybody, do you have any topics you'd like to talk about for the seminar?

Shunsuke: I'd love to learn more about pharmacy education in Asia.

Prof. Miller: OK, 5. _____.
(それを覚えておくよ)

Unit 1　Patient-Centered Communication in Pharmacy Practice

1.5 WRITING

次の日本語を英語に訳しなさい。

1. 薬物の物理的性質を知ることは、最良の投与経路を決定するために不可欠である。

　ヒント　物理的性質：physical nature　投与経路：route of administration

_____

_____

2. 薬物の作用機序を解明することはおもしろい。

　ヒント　作用機序：mechanism of action　解明する：elucidate

_____

_____

ホスピス発祥の国でみえたもの

　「医師にはこの治療が良いと言われた。でも薬剤師のあなただったらどうするか、教えてくれませんか」「空襲も必死の思いで逃れ今日まで生きてきた。あのときのような痛みはもう感じたくない」「モルヒネを使って頭がおかしくなりませんか。もうこの人と話せなくなりませんか」がん専門施設で働く私は、これまで沢山の患者さんやご家族の真剣に生と向き合う姿を見てきた。処方箋監査から調剤、服薬指導まで臨床薬剤師の仕事は多岐に渡る。その中でも、命にかかわる治療の決断を迫られる人々や最期の日々を送る人々には、薬学的な見解だけでなく、死生観や生き方に関わる対応を求められることも少なくない。

　3年前にホスピス発祥の国であるイギリスで、緩和ケアを学ぶ研修に参加した。セントクリストファーホスピスでランニングマシーンを使って運動しているご老人、患者さんではなく一人の人間として受け入れるロンドンのマギーズセンター*。イギリスで出会った人々が私の中に温かい火を灯してくれたような気がした。その人がこれまで歩んできた人生、今大切にしていることを尊重しながら、薬剤師という枠を超えて、患者さんに真に寄り添える存在でありたい。

　　　　　　　　　　　　　　　　　　　　　　　　　　　　　　　　　　沖﨑　歩

*2016年東京にもマギーズセンターが開設された。

7

Thalidomide: Tips for Entertainment Writers and Producers

UNIT 2

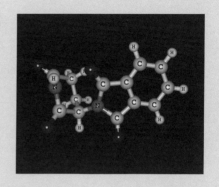

　米国保健福祉省（DHHS）所管の疾病予防管理センター（CDC）は、多くの米国人がテレビから健康情報を得ていることに着目し、番組制作者や脚本家向けに専門家の助言や知識、情報を公開している。ここでは、サリドマイドに関する情報を見る。この薬にはどんな問題があり、安全かつ効果的に使うにはどのような点に注意をすれば良いのか確認しよう。

READING

1-04

What's the Problem?

Taken early in pregnancy, thalidomide can cause devastating birth defects in children, most particularly shortened arms and legs, often with no elbows or knees. In spite of its tragic history of affecting more than 10,000 babies in Europe in the 1950's and 1960's when the risks were unknown, thalidomide has recently become available again (by prescription in the U.S. and over the counter in South America). In many cases, only one dose early in pregnancy can cause harmful effects.

Can It Be Prevented?

Yes. Thalidomide-affected pregnancies are completely preventable if proper precautions and guidelines are heeded. While it has been found to cause extreme malformations

birth defect
先天性欠損症、奇形

by prescription
処方薬として
over the counter
一般薬として

malformation
奇形

in unborn children, thalidomide also has a range of possible beneficial uses associated with fighting cancers, arthritis, tuberculosis, and many other diseases. Ironically, thalidomide's effectiveness at treating a wide range of illnesses may potentially make it more readily available to pregnant women, and therefore, a greater public health threat. Health care providers who prescribe thalidomide must ensure their female patients fully understand the need to avoid pregnancy while taking thalidomide. Health professionals also need to ensure a patient has a negative pregnancy test before writing a prescription for thalidomide.

unborn child
胎児

negative
陰性の

Tips for Scripts

- **INFORM** viewers that only one dose of thalidomide may cause a fetus to suffer devastating effects.

- **EDUCATE** viewers about the importance of following all warnings on drug labels, and to listen carefully to their doctors about precautions.

- **REMIND** women that over 50% of pregnancies are unplanned or mistimed, so a woman being treated with a potentially harmful drug should take extra precautions.

- **EXPLAIN** to viewers that thalidomide-affected pregnancies are completely preventable.

- **REASSURE** viewers that being aware of the risks of certain drugs and following all recommendations to eliminate such risks can lead to a successful treatment without harm to a pregnancy.

Case Examples

1. A parent who has a child affected by a thalidomide birth defect will likely feel guilt, shame, and a great sense of loss. In addition, a thalidomide-affected pregnancy can

cause conditions (such as a heart defect) that could lead to 45
the child's death shortly after birth. (If a child is to become
a regular part of this story, contact the Thalidomide
Victims Association of Canada for information about the
experiences and challenges of living with this disability.)
Several circumstances that can lead a pregnant woman 50
to unknowingly expose her baby to thalidomide can be
dramatized:

- A pharmacist makes an error in filling a prescription
  (potential litigation plot line).

- A health care provider writes a prescription for 55
  thalidomide but fails to tell the woman to avoid
  pregnancy while taking the drug.

- A pregnant woman with a drug dependency takes
  thalidomide from someone else's medicine cabinet.

- A woman who is trying to become pregnant is 60
  maliciously given thalidomide by someone who wants
  to cause harm to her baby.

- A woman taking thalidomide accidentally becomes
  pregnant as a result of contraceptive failure.

- A woman is given a prescription for thalidomide but 65
  fails to wait for the pregnancy test result (which is
  positive) before starting treatment.

2. A woman being treated with thalidomide seeks health
   information from the Internet; she discovers the
   many risks associated with teratogenic drugs such as 70
   thalidomide. Horrified by the potential for birth defects,
   and angered by the lack of information she received from
   her physician, she switches physicians immediately. She
   discusses the need for greater awareness and educational
   outreach among physicians. 75

Centers for Disease Control and Prevention (CDC) https://www.cdc.
gov/healthcommunication/toolstemplates/entertainmented/tips/
Thalidomide.html

Unit 2 Thalidomide: Tips for Entertainment Writers and Producers

2.1 COMPREHENSION QUESTIONS

Based on the passage, circle either T (true) or F (false) for each of the following statements.

1. If a woman takes thalidomide during pregnancy, in most cases her
    baby will be born dead. (T / F)

2. Only one dose of thalidomide early in pregnancy can cause harmful
    effects on a fetus. (T / F)

3. Thalidomide-affected pregnancies are completely preventable if health care
    providers who prescribe thalidomide ensure their female patients fully
    understand the need to avoid pregnancy while taking thalidomide. (T / F)

4. Thalidomide can cause devastating birth defects in children, such as
    shortened arms and legs, and heart defects. (T / F)

5. Pharmacists don't know enough about the benefits and risks of thalidomide
    to tell women to avoid pregnancy while taking the drug. (T / F)

2.2 PHARMACEUTICAL TERMINOLOGY

剤形に関する表現 (2)

　　ここでは外用薬の剤形を挙げている。bandageは一語だけでは「包帯」という意味
であるが、adhesiveと組み合わさるとどのような意味になるだろうか。

● 練習問題

*Match each of the following words with its definition below and then with its Japanese
translation (①-⑤).*

1. adhesive bandage (   ) [   ]   4. suppository   (   ) [   ]

2. poultice   (   ) [   ]   5. inhalant   (   ) [   ]

3. ointment   (   ) [   ]

(a) an aerosol or solvent medicine that is breathed in as a vapor

(b) a piece of absorbent gauze affixed to adhesive plastic or fabric for covering
wounds

(c) a smooth oily substance that is rubbed on the skin to heal a wound or sore
place

(d) a soft, moist mass of material applied to the body to relieve soreness and
inflammation and kept in place with a cloth

(e) a solid medical preparation in a roughly conical or cylindrical shape,
designed to be inserted into the rectum or vagina to dissolve

---

Japanese translations　　① 絆創膏　　② 吸入薬　　③ 坐薬　　④ 湿布薬　　⑤ 軟膏

11

2.3 GRAMMAR 「名詞」

　文の主要素になる名詞は、単数・複数の「数の一致」、および可算名詞・不可算名詞の区別が重要になる。また、名詞相当語句として、不定詞、動名詞、that節などがあることにも注意しよう。

● 練習問題

次の各文の誤りを正し、全文を日本語に訳しなさい。

1.　Approximately 6 million American adults have Alzheimer disease or mild cognitive impairment.

2.　These number will more than double to 15 million by 2060.

3.　Scientists across the United States and the world conduct wide-ranging researches to improve the health of our nation.

4.　Every moments of the day, your heart is pumping bloods throughout your body.

5.　Each cell nucleus contains 46 chromosomes in 23 pairs. These chromosomes pass on the genetic informations that makes us who we are.

Unit 2 Thalidomide: Tips for Entertainment Writers and Producers

2.4 LISTENING & SPEAKING

 1-05

Listen to the following conversation and fill in the blanks based on the Japanese.

In a seminar room.

Marina: So, last week we visited Nihon General Hospital and it was so interesting.

Shunsuke: 1. _____?
(特に何がおもしろかった？)

Marina: Well, the pharmacy was really big and there were so many pharmacists. 2. _____.
(30人よりたくさんいたと思います)

Shunsuke: That's a lot. When we visited a hospital in the UK, there were only four or five.

Marina: 3. _____
_____?
(イギリスの病院にも電子処方箋がありましたか)

Shunsuke: No. The pharmacy and use of prescriptions was really kind of old-fashioned—very low-tech.

Marina: 4. _____?
(ほかに違う点はありましたか？)

Shunsuke: Oh, everyone working in the hospital, except for the doctors, had a different color uniform.

Marina: What color was the pharmacists' uniform?

Shunsuke: They wore green uniforms. 5. _____
_____.
(看護師は青、一般スタッフは黄色を着ていた)
It was very colorful and different from a hospital in Japan.

13

2.5 WRITING

次の日本語を英語に訳しなさい。

1. 薬物動態の過程は、吸収、分布、代謝、排泄という4つの部分に分けることができる。

   ヒント 動態：disposition　吸収：absorption　分布：distribution　代謝：metabolism
   排泄：excretion

   _____

   _____

2. 舌下錠や経皮吸収型製剤を使うことによって、肝臓での初回通過効果を避けることができる。

   ヒント 舌下錠：sublingual tablet　経皮吸収型製剤：transdermal preparation
   初回通過効果：first-pass effect

   _____

   _____

ARTIST 時々 PHARMACIST

　日本で薬科大学と美術大学を卒業後、ドイツに留学した。日独韓を中心に、協働する仲間と共に制作活動を行っている。日本滞在中は、月単位の期間ではあるが、日本全国の薬局や病院で薬剤師として働くこともある。

　先日、日本の友人から「2007年上映されたテレビ映画『コンテルガン』がドイツの世論を動かし、製造元であるグリュネンタール社からドイツのサリドマイド被害者への謝罪と別途補償金を引出したとされるが、資料がほしい」と頼まれた。第2ドイツ放送（ZDF）やアーヘン地方新聞などがこのことを報じている。

　事実を科学的に証明することには限りがあり、より多面的に物事を見ることが重要である。AI（Artificial Intelligence）が世の中を席巻する社会では、人間の判断力、洞察力、クリエイティビティが再度問われる。Artistとして、時には医療人Pharmacistとして、別の領域を行き来しながら両方のクリティカルな視点を併せ持ち、目に見えない事実、心模様、変化などを芸術を通して表現したい。母語以外で他者とコミュニケーションができたとしても、人は何を話し、どう解釈できるかが結局は重要な要素だと、異文化の混在するドイツでの体験から学んだ。

　正しい情報に裏付けられた優れたエンターテイメントの持つ警鐘は今後も大いに期待できる。

大山　龍

FIP-WHO Technical Guidelines for Children-Specific Preparations

UNIT 3

2016年、世界保健機関と国際薬剤師・薬学連合は、小児用に使える承認薬がない場合に処方や供給に携わる医療従事者が安全かつ有効な小児薬を調合できるように、初の国際合意のガイドラインを発表した。小児医薬品の対象は新生児から思春期まで多様で幅広く、剤形や用量などは各年代に応じたきめ細かな対応が求められる。

READING

 1-06

Background

Paediatric patients should have access to authorized, age-appropriate preparations of medicines that can be administered safely and effectively. Nothing in this document
5　should detract from this objective. However, it is recognized that such preparations are not always available and in such cases a safe and effective alternative must be sought.

In the context of paediatric pharmacy practice, and for the purpose of this document, compounding is the technique
10　applied by pharmacists to produce medicines from active pharmaceutical ingredients (APIs) or using authorized medicines when no commercially available, authorized, age-appropriate or adequate dosage form exists.

Compared to the use of authorized medicines there are
15　significant risks associated with compounding; quality, safety and efficacy can rarely all be assured, and many errors have

FIP
国際薬剤師・薬学連合
（仏Fédération Internationale Pharmaceutique、英International Pharmaceutical Federation）
preparation 調製
paediatric = pediatric
（英）小児科の

compounding 調合

active pharmaceutical ingredient (API)
医薬品有効成分

bioavailability
バイオアベイラビリティ、生物学的利用能（投与された薬物が、どれだけ全身循環血中に到達し作用するかの指標）

manipulation 操作

therapeutic index
治療指数、治療係数（動物実験における薬物の50%致死量を50%有効量で除した値で、大きいほどその薬物は安全と考えられる）

dispersion
分散（液体中に薬物粒子を均一に存在させること）

excipient
賦形剤（固形製剤の製造において、増量、希釈、充填、補形の目的で用いられる添加物）

been reported in the preparation of such medicines. In some situations compounding of a medicine for a child may be the only option, which may be supported by evidence of quality and occasionally evidence of bioavailability by industry or other parties, such as academia. There may be alternatives to compounding, which should also be considered, for example, use of a commercially available therapeutic alternative or manipulation of authorized dosage forms.

This points-to-consider document is supported by a literature review of the evidence available. An annex to the report contains an update on the abstracts and papers published in 2010–2015.

Dose rounding

If the dose prescribed does not correspond to a dosage form that is commercially available, consider whether the dose can be suitably amended while maintaining safety and efficacy. The therapeutic index of the medicine and patient characteristics need to be considered before making a decision. Some medicine doses are calculated accurately on the basis of body weight, yet the therapeutic index is such that one dose can be used for a broad age and weight band. Consult the WHO Model formulary for children.

Manipulation of dosage forms

The practitioner should bear in mind that manipulation, such as tablet splitting, tablet/capsule dispersion, or tablet crushing and mixing with food or drink, may increase the potential for inaccurate dosing and may affect the efficacy, stability and bioavailability of the dosage form, in particular when mixed with food or drink. Excipients that are safe for adults may not necessarily be so for children.

16

When medicines are mixed with food or drink, including breast milk for very young children, an unpleasant tasting mixture may cause aversion in the child. In addition, the compatibility of the product with the food, drink or breast milk will need to be taken into account. Where a child shows signs of refusal or aversion other options should be considered.

compatibility　親和性

Oral liquids

APIs in compounded liquids may be susceptible to chemical reactions leading to degradation. The most common reactions are hydrolysis, oxidation and reduction. Usually the reaction rate or type is influenced by pH. Other factors that may increase the rate of reaction include the presence of trace metals which catalyse the oxidation of captopril, methyldopa or exposure to light, which catalyses the oxidative degradation of 6-mercaptopurine. The rate of chemical degradation usually increases with temperature.

Preparations made from tablets contain excipients such as binders and disintegrating agents in addition to the API. These excipients may reduce chemical stability by changing the pH to a value at which more rapid degradation occurs. This probably explains why amiloride solution prepared from pure API is more stable than an oral liquid prepared from tablets.

trace metal　微量金属

captopril　カプトプリル
（降圧薬、アンギオテンシン
変換酵素阻害薬）
methyldopa
メチルドパ（降圧薬）
oxidative degradation
酸化的分解
6-mercaptopurine
6-メルカプトプリン（抗腫瘍
薬、代謝拮抗薬、プリン代
謝阻害薬）
binder
結合剤（顆粒剤や錠剤など固
形製剤を構成する原料粒子
同士を結合させるための添加
物）
disintegrating agent
崩壊剤（錠剤などの固形製剤
が消化管液によって崩壊する
のを促すための添加物）
amiloride　アミロライド
（カリウム保持性利尿薬）

Annex 2 FIP-WHO technical guidelines: Points to consider in the provision by health-care professionals of children-specific preparations that are not available as authorized products http://www.fip.org/www/uploads/ database_file.php?id=375&table_id= p.88, p.92, p.93, p.98.

3.1 COMPREHENSION QUESTIONS

Fill in the blanks with appropriate words below based on the passage above.

(1.   ) and health professionals all over the world have long struggled with the lack of (2.   ) and commercially available (3.   ) medicines. They are often forced to use (4.   ) medicines when treating children, for example by crushing (5.   ) or making products from scratch. This approach poses significant (6.   ), increasing the potential for inaccurate dosing and impacting on the (7.   ), safety and efficacy of the medicine.

adult / quality / children-specific / risks / paediatricians / tablets / approved

3.2 PHARMACEUTICAL TERMINOLOGY

投薬・服薬に関する動詞

　「薬を飲む」という動詞は、水薬であっても"drink"ではなく、"take"である。投薬・服薬に関する動詞には以下の使い分けがある。take ([薬を] 飲む)、apply ([塗り薬を] 塗る、[貼り薬を] 貼る)、 put in (点眼する)、administer (投与する)、inject (注射する)、infuse* (注入する)。
* infuseは名詞形infusionで使われることが多い。

● 練習問題

Choose an appropriate verb for each type of medicine. You can use the same verb twice.

1. (　　　)　a tablet

2. (　　　)　syrup

3. (　　　)　ointment

4. (　　　)　IV fluids

5. (　　　)　eye drops

(a) take   **(b)** apply   **(c)** put in   **(d)** administer

Unit 3　FIP-WHO Technical Guidelines for Children-Specific Preparations

3.3 GRAMMAR 「形容詞」

　　形容詞には、名詞を修飾する限定用法と、主格補語、目的格補語になる叙述用法がある。名詞を修飾する形容詞の位置によって、前位の形容、後位の形容があり、英語の文情報を多彩に彩る後位の形容を習得することが肝要である。また、形容詞相当語句として、分詞、不定詞、前置詞句、関係代名詞節などがあることにも注意しよう。

● 練習問題

次の各文の（　）内の選択肢から適切なものを選び、全文を日本語に訳しなさい。

1.　DNA is a nucleic acid (**make** / **making** / **made**) of bonded strings of nucleotides with a backbone of phosphate and deoxyribose.

　　（　　　　　　　　）

　　_____

　　_____

2.　The letters of the DNA alphabet make sentences, (**know** / **knowing** / **known**) as genes, which tell your cells what to do.

　　（　　　　　　　　）

　　_____

3.　Humans share 98.5 percent of their DNA with chimpanzees, but that little bit of genetic code (**it** / **that** / **whose**) is different is what makes us unique.

　　（　　　　　　　　）

　　_____

　　_____

4.　Every human (**in** / **on** / **for**) the planet shares 99.9 percent of the same DNA.

　　（　　　　　　　　）

　　_____

5.　People (**of** / **in** / **with**) diabetes can't make their own insulin and can become very sick.

　　（　　　　　　　　）

　　_____

3.4 LISTENING & SPEAKING

 1-07

Listen to the following conversation and fill in the blanks based on the Japanese.

In a seminar room.

Prof. Miller: Good morning, everyone! I hope you had a nice weekend. Today, I want to talk about the 1. _____

_____.

（国際薬学生連盟）

Masayuki: What's that? And how do we find out more information?

Prof. Miller: Good questions, Masayuki! The IPSF started in 1949 in London. 2. _____,

（初めのうちはどちらかというと小規模だった）

but now there are almost 350,000 student members in 80 different countries. They have a homepage.

Masayuki: Can you tell us the URL? I would like to learn more about this group.

Prof. Miller: Sure! It is www.ipsf.org. There is no Japanese, 3. _____

_____.

（だから君たちには英語をがんばってほしい）

Masayuki: I will! This sounds so interesting.

Prof. Miller: They have an annual conference for students, in fact. A few years ago the conference was here in Japan. 4. _____

_____. Are you on Facebook?

（フェイスブックページもある）

Masayuki: Yes, I am. I will look for their page on Facebook now. Is that OK?

Prof. Miller: Sure. I hope you join. 5. _____

_____.

（それは君が自分の英語を使うのによい方法だ）

Unit 3　FIP-WHO Technical Guidelines for Children-Specific Preparations

3.5 WRITING

次の日本語を英語に訳しなさい。

1. 毒物学は薬理学の一部門であり、生体に対する化学物質の有害作用を扱う。

   ヒント 毒物学：toxicology　有害作用：adverse effect

   _____

   _____

2. この研究室では、薬物と内因性物質との相互作用を研究している。

   ヒント 内因性物質：endogenous substance

   _____

   _____

非がん非ターミナルの小児の在宅医療

　医療が進歩するに伴い子どもの死亡率は著しく低下したが、その一方で重篤な状態を脱しても薬物療法の継続が必要な子どもたちは増えている。特に重症の場合は人工的な呼吸管理や栄養管理が必要となり、これらの医療を継続するために子どもたちは入院し続けざるを得なかった。しかし、地域の在宅医療とそのための薬物供給の仕組みが整い、病院での医療を継続しながら自宅で暮らせるようになりつつある。

　この子たちにとっての在宅医療は、いわゆる「看取り」が着地点とは限らない。これから成長し、教育を受けていく途上にある。これが高齢者の在宅医療との大きな違いだと感じる。客観的に見れば厳しい状況でも、いつか新しく画期的な医療技術が見つかったら、この子は笑うかも入れない、立ち上がるかもしれない、学校に通って、社会に出て…と、親たちは諦めていない。命を繋いで、いつかそういう日が来るかもしれないと、どこかで希望を持ち続けている。

　様々な困難な状況を経て生きるという運命を与えられた子どもたちと、悲嘆と葛藤を繰り返しながらも家で育てると覚悟を決めた家族が、その人たちらしく生きることを支援する。それが小児在宅医療のあるべき姿ではないだろうか。

　　　　　　　　　　　　　　　　　　　　　　　　　　　　　川名三知代

Dioxins and Their Effects on Human Health

UNIT 4

　ダイオキシン類は意図せずに生成する化合物であり、塩素を含む物質の不完全燃焼や化学合成の際の副産物である。ダイオキシン類の中でもTCDDには強い毒性があり、生殖器官に対する毒性や発がん性などが指摘されている。TCDDと似た構造をもち同様の毒性を示す化合物を総称してダイオキシン類と呼ぶ。

READING

 1-08

Key Facts

- Dioxins are a group of chemically-related compounds that are persistent organic pollutants (POPs).

- Dioxins are found throughout the world in the environment and they accumulate in the food chain, mainly in the fatty tissue of animals.

- More than 90% of human exposure is through food, mainly meat and dairy products, fish and shellfish. Many national authorities have programmes in place to monitor the food supply.

- Dioxins are highly toxic and can cause reproductive and developmental problems, damage the immune system, interfere with hormones and also cause cancer.

- Due to the omnipresence of dioxins, all people have background exposure, which is not expected to affect

persistent 残留性の

food chain 食物連鎖
fatty tissue 脂肪組織

immune system 免疫系

omnipresence 遍在

human health. However, due to the highly toxic potential, efforts need to be undertaken to reduce current background exposure.

- Prevention or reduction of human exposure is best done via source-directed measures, i.e. strict control of industrial processes to reduce formation of dioxins.

Background

Dioxins are environmental pollutants. They belong to the so-called "dirty dozen"—a group of dangerous chemicals known as persistent organic pollutants (POPs). Dioxins are of concern because of their highly toxic potential. Experiments have shown they affect a number of organs and systems.

Once dioxins enter the body, they last a long time because of their chemical stability and their ability to be absorbed by fat tissue, where they are then stored in the body. Their half-life in the body is estimated to be 7 to 11 years. In the environment, dioxins tend to accumulate in the food chain. The higher an animal is in the food chain, the higher the concentration of dioxins.

The chemical name for dioxin is: 2,3,7,8-tetrachlorodibenzo-para-dioxin (TCDD). The name "dioxins" is often used for the family of structurally and chemically related polychlorinated dibenzo-para-dioxins (PCDDs) and polychlorinated dibenzofurans (PCDFs). Certain dioxin-like polychlorinated biphenyls (PCBs) with similar toxic properties are also included under the term "dioxins". Some 419 types of dioxin-related compounds have been identified but only about 30 of these are considered to have significant toxicity, with TCDD being the most toxic.

dirty dozen
ダーティー・ダズン（12種類の汚染物質）

half-life 半減期

2,3,7,8-tetrachlorodibenzo-para-dioxin
2,3,7,8-テトラクロロジベンゾパラジオキシン

polychlorinated dibenzo-para-dioxin (PCDD)
ポリクロロジベンゾパラジオキシン

polychlorinated dibenzofuran (PCDF)
ポリクロロジベンゾフラン

Effects of dioxins on human health

chloracne
塩素挫瘡（有機塩素化合物の慢性影響の結果として現れるにきび様の皮疹）

patchy darkening
斑状の黒ずみ

Short-term exposure of humans to high levels of dioxins may result in skin lesions, such as chloracne and patchy darkening of the skin, and altered liver function. Long-term exposure is linked to impairment of the immune system, the developing nervous system, the endocrine system and reproductive functions.

International Agency for Research on Cancer (IARC)
国際がん研究機関

Chronic exposure of animals to dioxins has resulted in several types of cancer. TCDD was evaluated by the WHO's International Agency for Research on Cancer (IARC) in 1997 and 2012. Based on animal data and on human epidemiology data, TCDD was classified by IARC as a "known human carcinogen". However, TCDD does not affect genetic material and there is a level of exposure below which cancer risk would be negligible.

body burden 体内負荷

Due to the omnipresence of dioxins, all people have background exposure and a certain level of dioxins in the body, leading to the so-called body burden. Current normal background exposure is not expected to affect human health on average. However, due to the high toxic potential of this class of compounds, efforts need to be undertaken to reduce current background exposure.

WHO http://www.who.int/mediacentre/factsheets/fs225/en/

Unit 4 Dioxins and Their Effects on Human Health

4.1 COMPREHENSION QUESTIONS

Based on the passage, circle either T (true) or F (false) for each of the following statements.

1. Dioxins are persistent in the body for a long time. (T / F)

2. So far, we have identified around 800 dioxin-related compounds. (T / F)

3. Polychlorinated dibenzo-para-dioxins (PCDDs) are considered to be the most toxic of dioxins. (T / F)

4. TCDD is regarded as a cancer-causing compound. (T / F)

5. Dioxins exist extensively in the environment. (T / F)

4.2 PHARMACEUTICAL TERMINOLOGY

調剤業務に関する動詞

　日本語では「処方箋を調剤する」「薬を調剤する」と言うが、英語では目的語がprescriptionかmedicationかによって異なる動詞が使われる。

● 練習問題

Choose an appropriate verb for each type of medicine according to the meaning in Japanese.

1. (　　　) medicines 　　　薬を処方する

2. (　　　) a prescription 　　処方箋を調剤する

3. (　　　) medication 　　　薬を調剤する

4. (　　　) medications 　　（特定の患者のために）薬を調合する

5. (　　　) medications 　　薬を保管する

(a) compound　　**(b)** dispense　　**(c)** fill　　**(d)** prescribe　　**(e)** store

---

25

4.3 GRAMMAR 「動詞」

　英語の動詞には、目的語をとる他動詞と、目的語をとらない自動詞がある。他動詞は、受動態（受身）になれる動詞である。また、動詞が副詞や前置詞などと共起して句動詞（phrasal verb）として1語の動詞と同じ働きをすることがある。文構造上、英語はSVO言語、日本語はSOV言語といわれ、動詞の位置が日本人学習者を惑わす要因でもある。

● 練習問題

次の各文の誤りを正し、全文を日本語に訳しなさい。

1. Neurons are specializing to transmit signals throughout the body.

2. Interneurons receive information transmit by other neurons and then transmit the same information to any other neuron.

3. Do you know how a certain smell can remind you old memories?

4. Billions of neurons receives electrical impulses from nerves in your body.

5. Faster than the fastest computer, your amazing brain controls every move you to make.

Unit 4 Dioxins and Their Effects on Human Health

4.4 LISTENING & SPEAKING

Listen to the following conversation and fill in the blanks based on the Japanese.

In a lecture room.

Prof. Hayashi: Thank you so much for your wonderful lecture today, Dr. Adams!

Dr. Adams: It was my pleasure. I just hope I didn't speak too fast.

Prof. Suzuki: 1. _____.
(ちょうど良い早さで話してくださったと思います)
Having said that, let's see if today's participants have any questions.
2. _____.
(質問がある人は、遠慮しないで聞いてください)

Yuria: I have a question. Dr. Adams, you said that the pharmacy students in America have to do a hospital practice from their first year.
3. _____?
(実習はどのくらいの期間やるのですか)

Dr. Adams: Yes, they have a hospital practice for one month. Before that they have to study hard, then they have OSCEs where we evaluate their communication skills. 4. _____,
(学生はOSCEに合格した後で)
they can go to their hospital practice.

Yuria: I see. We have OSCEs, too, but not until our fourth year. What do the students do in their hospital practice?

Dr. Adams: 5. _____
_____ and then they will go on rounds
(先輩の薬学生が調剤に関して彼らを指導するでしょう)
together in a ward. It will be very hands-on.

Yuria: Thank you for your answer. I understand and it sounds very interesting!

27

4.5 WRITING

次の日本語を英語に訳しなさい。

1. 薬剤開発において、私たちはときどき利益相反に直面する。

   ヒント 利益相反：conflict of interest

   _____

   _____

2. 薬剤スクリーニングの過程で、予期しなかった治療効果がときおり発見される。

   ヒント 治療効果：therapeutic effect

   _____

   _____

前向きに考えることの大切さ

　2018年1月から半年間、カリフォルニア州にあるスタンフォード大学化学科で研究を行った。そこで最も印象に残ったことは何事も前向きに捉えること。例えば、実験がなかなか進展しない際にも、まず「それはいいことを試した」から話が始まり、一歩でも研究が進むように前向きなディスカッションが続く。研究室間では試薬類や実験器具の貸し借りが自由で、学部を越えた共同研究も盛んだ。さらに外部講師を招くセミナーが頻繁に開催され、驚くことに化学科だけでも年間100回を超える。講師は発表前後に複数の研究室を訪問し大学院生とディスカッションをする機会を持つ。研究の世界は意外と狭いもので、このような場での繋がりが将来にとり大切になるかもしれない。定期開催の研究室内ミーティングでは次々と質問が出され、何より疑問点をその場で解決する姿勢が尊敬できる。この積極性は日本にいる場合と少々異なり学ぶべきものと感じる。新しい課題に直面した際に日本のやり方しか知らない場合には他の選択肢になかなか気付くことができないが、外国のやり方も知ることで様々な選択肢の中から解決策を選ぶことができる。海外では現地の言葉、文化、習慣を学ぶことができるし、たくさんの刺激が待っている。勇気を持って日本を飛び出してみては！

齋藤弘明

Disorders of Amino Acid Metabolism

UNIT 5

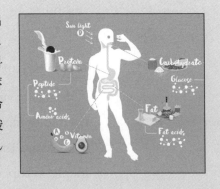

私たちが毎日摂る食事からエネルギーを作り出す過程を代謝と言う。消化器官は、食物を分解して糖や酸などの体を動かす燃料にする。この燃料はすぐに使え、また体の中にエネルギーとして蓄えることができる。代謝がうまくいかないと生命に支障をきたす。そうした障害の一つにアミノ酸代謝異常症がある。アミノ酸代謝異常症とはどんな疾患なのか学んでみよう。

READING

Amino acids are the building blocks of proteins and have many functions in the body. Hereditary disorders of amino acid processing can result from defects either in the breakdown of amino acids or in the body's ability to get amino acids into
5   cells. Because these disorders cause symptoms early in life, newborns are routinely screened for several common ones. In the United States, newborns are commonly screened for phenylketonuria, maple syrup urine disease, homocystinuria, tyrosinemia, and a number of other inherited disorders,
10 although screening varies from state to state.

Phenylketonuria (PKU)

PKU occurs in infants born without the ability to normally break down an amino acid called phenylalanine. Phenylalanine, which is toxic to the brain, builds up in the
15 blood. PKU is a disorder that causes a buildup of the amino

newborn
新生児
routinely
ルーチンで（ルーチンとは、各個人に合わせるのではなく対象者に対して必ず行われる基本的な手順）
inherited disorder
遺伝性疾患、遺伝病

essential amino acid
必須アミノ酸

intellectual disability
知的障害

by-product 副産物

dialysis 透析

decreased vision
視力減退(低下)

acid phenylalanine, which is an essential amino acid that cannot be synthesized in the body but is present in food. Excess phenylalanine is normally converted to tyrosine, another amino acid, and eliminated from the body. Without the enzyme that converts it to tyrosine, phenylalanine builds 20 up in the blood and is toxic to the brain, causing an intellectual disability.

Maple Syrup Urine Disease

Maple syrup urine disease is caused by lack of the enzyme needed to metabolize amino acids. By-products of these amino 25 acids cause the urine to smell like maple syrup. Children with maple syrup urine disease are unable to metabolize certain amino acids. By-products of these amino acids build up, causing neurologic changes, including seizures and intellectual disability. These by-products also cause body fluids, such as 30 urine and sweat, to smell like maple syrup. Since 2007, nearly every state in the United States has required that all newborns be screened for maple syrup urine disease with a blood test. Infants with severe disease are treated with dialysis. Some children with mild disease benefit from injections of vitamin 35 B$_1$ (thiamin). After the disease has been brought under control, children must always consume a special artificial diet that is low in three amino acids (leucine, isoleucine, and valine).

Homocystinuria

Homocystinuria is caused by lack of the enzyme needed 40 to metabolize homocysteine. This disorder can cause a number of symptoms, including decreased vision and skeletal abnormalities. Infants with this disorder are normal at birth. The first symptoms, including dislocation of the lens of the eye, causing severely decreased vision, usually begin after 45

Unit 5 Disorders of Amino Acid Metabolism

3 years of age. Most children have skeletal abnormalities, including osteoporosis. Children are usually tall and thin with a curved spine, chest deformities, elongated limbs, and long, spiderlike fingers. Without early diagnosis and treatment, mental (psychiatric) and behavioral disorders and intellectual disability are common. Since 2008, nearly every state in the United States has required that all newborns be screened for homocystinuria with a blood test. A test measuring enzyme function in liver or skin cells confirms the diagnosis. Some children with homocystinuria improve when given vitamin B_6 (pyridoxine) or vitamin B_{12} (cobalamin).

osteoporosis
骨粗しょう症

Tyrosinemia

Tyrosinemia is caused by lack of the enzyme needed to metabolize tyrosine. The most common form of this disorder mostly affects the liver and the kidneys. Children with tyrosinemia are unable to completely metabolize the amino acid tyrosine. By-products of this amino acid build up, causing a variety of symptoms. In some states, the disorder is detected with newborn screening tests.

https://www.merckmanuals.com/home/children-s-health-issues/
hereditary-metabolic-disorders/disorders-of-amino-acid-metabolism

5.1 COMPREHENSION QUESTIONS

Based on the passage, circle either T (true) or F (false) for each of the following statements.

1. PKU is caused by lack of the enzyme needed to convert phenylalanine
   to cysteine. (T / F)

2. Children with PKU are unable to metabolize a certain essential
   amino acid. (T / F)

3. The diagnoses of PKU, maple syrup urine disease, and homocystinuria
   are based on a blood test. (T / F)

4. Children with maple syrup urine disease have urine and sweat with a
   distinctive maple syrup odor. (T / F)

5. PKU, maple syrup urine disease, and homocystinuria disorders are
   usually hereditary diseases. (T / F)

5.2 PHARMACEUTICAL TERMINOLOGY

医薬用語に使われる接頭辞 (1)

　医学・薬学英語において接頭辞・接尾辞を学ぶことは非常に重要である。用語の多くが接頭辞＋語根＋接尾辞によって構成されているからである。一般英語での接頭辞a-には「非、無」以外の意味もあるが、医薬英語では「非、無」という意味のみで使われる。

① a-, an- (= not, without)　② anti- (= against)　③ contra- (= against)

④ dis- (= absence, removal, separation)

● 練習問題

Write the meanings of the word parts and then of the whole given words in Japanese.

1. analgesic
   an- _____　　　-algia _____　　(　　　　　)

2. antiemetic
   anti- _____　　　emetic _____　　(　　　　　)

3. antidiarrheal
   anti- _____　　　diarrhea _____　　(　　　　　)

4. contraindication
   contra- _____　　　indication _____　　(　　　　　)

5. disinfectant
   dis- _____　　　infectant _____　　(　　　　　)

Unit 5 Disorders of Amino Acid Metabolism

5.3 GRAMMAR 「副詞」

　　副詞は、形容詞、副詞、動詞、文全体を修飾する働きをする。また、副詞は、-ly の語尾に代表される一語からなるものの他に、前置詞句、不定詞句、分詞句や節の形をとり、同様の働きをするものがある。効果的な副詞の活用は、美文を作るだけでなく、知性、人柄のバロメータにもなりうる。

● 練習問題

次の各文の誤りを正し、全文を日本語に訳しなさい。

1. Bright colored fruits and vegetables are especially good for you.

2. The Chinese government lately banned the sale of GM rice in China to avoid making their population sick, while exporting it to many other countries.

3. The oil keeps the engine clean and kindness keeps things running smooth.

4. The gall bladder and pancreas send juices to the intestines to help digestion.

5. The doctor can see the intestines in an x-ray.

5.4 LISTENING & SPEAKING

 1-11

Listen to the following conversation and fill in the blanks based on the Japanese.

In a restaurant after the special lecture by Dr. Adams.

Prof. Hayashi: Thank you so much for a wonderful lecture today, Dr. Adams!

Dr. Adams: It was my pleasure. The students had lots of questions. 1. _____

_____.

（質問に答えることができて非常にうれしかったです）

Prof. Hayashi: They did, indeed. Oh, before I forget, 2. _____

_____? Preferences?

（食物アレルギーはありますか）

Dr. Adams: Nope. I eat almost anything. 3. _____

_____!

（私は特に和食が大好きです）

Prof. Hayashi: Well, this is a famous crab restaurant. I think you will like it, but every dish will have some crab in it. 4. _____

_____?

（カニにうんざりしてしまうかもしれませんね）

Dr. Adams: Oh, please don't worry! I almost never get to eat crab in America. It is quite expensive. It seems cheaper here.

Prof. Hayashi: Is that so? I thought America was cheaper than here in Japan.

Dr. Adams: Actually, it seems that the prices are cheap here. 5. _____

_____?

（それに、チップを渡さないのですよね？）

Prof. Hayashi: That's right. We don't have to tip tonight.

Unit 5　Disorders of Amino Acid Metabolism

5.5 WRITING

次の日本語を英語に訳しなさい。

1. 製造販売の前に、製薬会社は薬の安全性および有効性を証明しなくてはならない。

   ヒント　製造販売：marketing　有効性：efficacy

   _____

   _____

2. 現在、私は医薬情報担当者として働いているが、将来は自分のコンピューターの知識が使える薬剤設計チームに加わりたい。

   ヒント　医薬情報担当者：medical representative

   _____

   _____

国際交流から日本の麻酔管理の未来を目指して

　米国では約150年も前から手術や麻酔管理の安全と充実のために麻酔看護師（Certified Registered Nurse Anesthetist: CRNA）という資格がある。日本ではそのような資格はないが、患者の高齢化・病態の複雑化により、外科手術件数は増加し、麻酔科医師の他に麻酔管理ができる看護師が病院の認定で協働している。

　2018年、日米で麻酔管理を実施する看護師の交流会が初めて日本で開催された。もちろんコミュニケーションの言語は英語である。米国は長い歴史的背景があり、麻酔看護師の役割は発展し、手術を受ける患者に対し麻酔管理の安全は充実している。これまでの米国のその成果を論文で読んだが、やはり同様だ。すばらしい。しかし、最先端の米国でも論文ではみえない日本と同様の困難があることが交流を通してわかった。この事実は英語でのコミュニケーションがはかれたからこそ見えた事実だ。英語で国際交流できることは、事実が確認でき、視野がより広がり、医療職としての仕事の深さや幅の広さにつながる。日本の麻酔管理も薬のスペシャリストである薬剤師が協働し、一緒に国際交流していく未来を私は楽しみにしている。

赤瀬智子

35

The Body's Second Line of Defence

UNIT 6

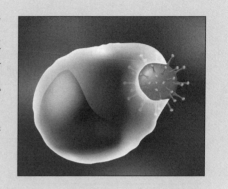

感染に対して我々の体は生体防御機構を備えている。生体防御機構の第一線（第1防御線）は皮膚などの物理的障壁である。これが破られた場合は、第2防御線が始動する。体内の様々な免疫細胞が、侵入してきた病原体を攻撃し、感染を抑えようとするのである。ここでは、免疫システムの基礎を解説したニュージーランドの科学学習サイトの記事を読んでみよう。

READING

1-12

pathogen 病原体
first line of defence 防御の第一線、第1防御線

immune response 免疫応答

disease-causing organism 病原生物（病気を引き起こす生物）

neutrophil 好中球
pawn ポーン（チェスの駒の一種。将棋の「歩」にあたる）

If the pathogens are able to get past the first line of defence, for example, through a cut in your skin, and an infection develops, the second line of defence becomes active. Through a sequence of steps called the immune response, the immune system attacks these pathogens.

The second line of defence is a group of cells, tissues and organs that work together to protect the body. This is the immune system.

Cells

The cells involved are white blood cells (leukocytes), which seek out and destroy disease-causing organisms or substances. There are different types of leukocytes. Each of these cell types has a specific function, but they all work together to protect you.

Neutrophils: These cells primarily attack bacteria. They are dispensable, rather like pawns on a chessboard. They rush to the site of incoming bacteria to fight them, but are easily killed.

Neutrophils only last a few days in the body (before they self-destruct), but our bone marrow produces more every day.

bone marrow 骨髄

20 **T helper cells:** These cells are like the bosses. They give instructions to other cells by producing signals. Each T helper cell only looks out for one type of pathogen.

Cytotoxic (killer) T cells: These are killer cells. They punch holes in the walls of the pathogen cell so that the contents ooze
25 out.

cytotoxic (killer) T cell
細胞傷害性（キラー）T細胞

Macrophages: Macrophage means 'big eater'. These cells 'eat' (ingest) or clean up the mess of dead cells.

Dendritic cells: These cells are like the spies. They notice if there is an invader and then present evidence of the invader to
30 T cells in the lymph nodes.

dendritic cell 樹状細胞

lymph node リンパ節

B cells: These produce antibodies, which lock onto the antigen of invading bacteria and immobilise them until the macrophage consumes them.

The tissues and organs

35 The tissues and organs involved in the immune system are the lymphatic system, lymph nodes and lymph fluid.

lymphatic system
リンパ系
lymph fluid リンパ液

How it works

When a pathogen invades the body, the neutrophils gather at the entry site and try to engulf it and destroy it. Should the
40 invaders get past the neutrophils, several things may happen. The macrophages will be attracted by the death throes of the neutrophils. These cells attempt to engulf the invader, but they also send signals to other cells for help.

throe 激痛

The dendritic cells, which are constantly scouting around
45 may find the pathogen and take a piece to present to T helper cells that congregate in the lymph nodes in the body.

scout around 探し回る

present 提示する

A T helper cell will recognise only one pathogen. If the T helper cell recognises the invader, it will immediately clone

clone クローンする、
コピーする

to increase numbers. The T helper cell then activates the
appropriate immune cells for the attack.

If the invading organism is a virus, the T helper cell will
signal the cytotoxic (killer) T cells to come to the rescue. These
cells punch holes in the walls of invading virus-infected host
cells, killing the cells and destroying the virus. B cells can
also be activated to produce antibodies that will stick to free
viruses, marking them out for macrophages to clean up.

If the invader is bacterial, B cells are usually drawn to
the task. They squirt an antibody (IgG) onto the bacteria.
This sticks everything together and makes it attractive to
macrophages, which clear up the mess.

virus-infected
ウイルスに感染した
host cell 宿主細胞

free virus 遊離ウイルス

squirt 吹き掛ける
IgG (= immunoglobulin G)
免疫グロブリンＧ

T helper cell response to virus infection

T helper cell

Once the T helper cell detects a virus fragment it activates and divides (clonal expansion). Some stay as memory cells. Others respond as shown.

Calming cytokines (proteins)

Cytokines (activating proteins)

Cytokines (activating proteins)

Cytokines (activating proteins)

Cytokines (activating proteins)

Cytokines (activating proteins)

Suppressor T cells are stimulated to slow down immune response once virus is cleared.

Killer T cells are activated to kill virus infected cells.

Macrophages are stimulated to become more effective at clearing debris.

B cells are stimulated to produce antibodies which stick to free virus.

Virus infected cells   Antibody coated virus

Notes: Viruses are not to scale – they are much, much smaller.

cytokine サイトカイン
clonal expansion
クローン増殖

Immune response is extremely complex. This illustration focuses on some ways T helper cells respond to virus infection. The T helper cell communicates with many cells, giving instructions to destroy the virus.

The body's second line of defence https://www.sciencelearn.org.nz/
resources/178-the-body-s-second-line-of-defence

Unit 6 The Body's Second Line of Defence

6.1 COMPREHENSION QUESTIONS

Answer the following questions in English.

1. Why can we usually keep pathogens out of the body?

    _____

2. There are different types of leukocytes. What would happen to our immune
    system, if one of the leukocytes stopped functioning? Why?

    _____

3. What kills neutrophils?

    _____

4. How do B cells and macrophages collaborate to get rid of bacteria from the
    body? Explain in your own words.

    _____

5. Make a sentence using the phrase "scout around."

    _____

6.2 PHARMACEUTICAL TERMINOLOGY

医薬用語に使われる接頭辞 (2)

　接頭辞、接尾辞を知っていると、一見難しく見える医学・薬学英単語の意味も容易
に推測することができる。inter-とよく似た接頭辞にintra-(= within, inside)があるの
で、混同しないように注意しよう（Unit 7参照）。

① hyper- (= over, above)　　② hypo- (= under, below)　　③ inter- (= between)
④ pre- (= before)

● 練習問題

*Translate the following terms into Japanese paying attention to the meaning of the
prefixes.*

1. hypotensive　　　_____

2. hypoglycemic　　_____

3. interaction　　　_____

4. prediabetic　　　_____

5. prevention　　　_____

39

6.3 GRAMMAR 「接続詞」

接続詞は、語、句、節、文を結びつける働きをする。その用法には等位接続詞と従位接続詞がある。類似した働きをするものとして、both A and B; not only A but also B; A as well as B; either A or Bなどがある。

● **練習問題**

次の各文の誤りを正し、全文を日本語に訳しなさい。

1. Blood carries oxygen and nutrients to all the cells in your body so they can grow but stay healthy.

2. Blood is made up of four parts—plasma, red cells, white cells, platelets.

3. When a virus enters your body, white blood cells rush to destroy the virus if you get better.

4. If you break a bone, it can grow together again even though you keep it still. That's why you might have to wear a cast.

5. How long can you keep certain foods in the fridge after they become unsafe to eat?

   ヒント 消費期間は？

Unit 6　The Body's Second Line of Defence

6.4 LISTENING & SPEAKING

 1-13

Listen to the following conversation and fill in the blanks based on the Japanese.

In a seminar room.

Prof. Tanaka:　Hello, do you mind if I ask a favor?

Prof. Miller:　Not at all. 1._____?
　　　　　　　　　　　　　　（どんなご用件ですか）

Prof. Tanaka:　Well, we had to translate the model core curriculum from Japanese into English and 2._____
_____.
　　　　　　　（私たちにはわからない部分がいくつかあります）

Prof. Miller:　You want me to have a look? 3._____?
　　　　　　　　　　　　　（そしてフィードバックを与えるということですか）

Prof. Tanaka:　If you can, that would help us a lot. See this sentence, 4._____
_____?
　　　　　　　（これは意味が通じますか）

Prof. Miller:　This refers to the female reproductive system. Where is the mention of the male reproductive system?

Prof. Tanaka:　Actually that is a great point! The original Japanese just says reproductive system. I guess we thought it was meant just for women.

Prof. Miller:　Well, men have one, too. (laughs) But the rest of the sentences look good to me.

Prof. Tanaka:　Thank you so much! 5._____
_____.
　　　　　　（メモを取ってこの文章を直します）

41

6.5 WRITING

次の日本語を英語に訳しなさい。

1. 薬の作用時間は、薬の用量や半減期など、多数の要因により決まる。

   ヒント 作用時間：duration of action　用量：dose　半減期：half-life

   _____

   _____

2. 動物実験においては、治療指数は通常、試験している薬のTD$_{50}$対ED$_{50}$の比と定義される。

   ヒント 治療指数：therapeutic index

   _____

   _____

英語版薬学教育モデル・コアカリキュラム（平成25年度改訂版）公開

　2018年3月、Model Core Curriculum for Pharmacy Education (2013 Version) が完成し、公益社団法人日本薬学会ウェブサイトに掲載された。日本の薬学コアカリをなぜ英語で公開しなくてはならないのだろうか？

　2006年4月、薬剤師養成を目的とする薬学教育課程が6年に延長され、同時にナショナルスタンダードとしての薬学コアカリが導入された。2015年からは改訂コアカリにより、新しい薬学教育が展開されている。

　英語版コアカリ改訂版のPreface(序文)によれば、"Japan will continue efforts to ensure that its education system, curriculum content, and knowledge taught meet or exceed international standards. …consistent with the WHO 8-star pharmacist…"とある。日本が目指すのは、2000年(「研究者」は2006年に追加)に世界保健機関が提唱した国際標準"8つ星薬剤師"(「ケア提供者(Caregiver)」、「意思決定者(Decision-maker)」、「情報提供者(Communicator)」、「管理者(Manager)」、「生涯学習者(Life-long learner)」、「教育者(Teacher)」、「指導者(Leader)」、「研究者(Researcher)」)の養成である。

　日本の薬学教育は世界標準？　海外の薬学教育は？　インターネットを利用すれば、情報は容易に入手できるし、問い合わせもできる。ただ、その内容を正確に理解するためには、その国の社会制度や文化などの背景知識も必要だ。英語版コアカリが公開された。これを使って、自分が学んでいることを海外の薬学生に伝えてみよう！　どんな反応が戻ってくるだろう!?

堀内正子

Foodborne Germs and Illness

UNIT 7

急な腹痛や下痢、嘔吐などの症状が出ると疑われるのが「食品媒介疾患」、いわゆる食中毒である。衛生管理の整った日本では食中毒の発生は徐々に減ってきているが、まだ高い頻度で発生して毎年多くの患者が出ている。海外では衛生事情が異なるため、細菌性の食中毒は特に注意が必要な感染症である。ここでは、「食品媒介疾患」の原因が何であるかを探り、どのような過程を経て発症するのかをそれぞれ予防も考慮しながら確認していこう。

READING

1-14

　Foodborne illness (sometimes called "foodborne disease," "foodborne infection," or "food poisoning") is a common, costly—yet preventable—public health problem. Each year, 1 in 6 Americans gets sick by consuming contaminated foods
5 or beverages. More than 250 different foodborne diseases have been described. Most of these diseases are infections, caused by a variety of bacteria, viruses, and parasites that can be foodborne. Other diseases are poisonings, caused by harmful toxins or chemicals that have contaminated the
10 food, for example, poisonous mushrooms. These different diseases have many different symptoms, so there is no one "syndrome" that is foodborne illness. However, the microbe or toxin enters the body through the gastrointestinal tract, and often causes the first symptoms there, so nausea, vomiting,
15 abdominal cramps and diarrhea are common symptoms in

gastrointestinal tract
胃腸管

abdominal cramp
腹部疝痛

many foodborne diseases.

There are many opportunities for food to become contaminated as it is produced and prepared. Many foodborne microbes are present in healthy animals (usually in their intestines) that are raised for food. Meat and poultry carcasses can become contaminated during slaughter by contact with small amounts of intestinal contents. Similarly, fresh fruits and vegetables can be contaminated if they are washed or irrigated with water that is contaminated with animal manure or human sewage. Some types of *Salmonella* can infect a hen's ovary so that the internal contents of a normal looking egg can be contaminated with *Salmonella* even before the shell is formed. Oysters and other filter feeding shellfish can concentrate *Vibrio* bacteria that are naturally present in sea water, or other microbes such as norovirus that are present in human sewage dumped into the sea.

Later in food processing, other foodborne microbes can be introduced from infected humans who handle the food, or by cross contamination from some other raw agricultural product. In the kitchen, microbes can be transferred from one food to another food by using the same knife, cutting board, or other utensil to prepare both, without washing the surface or utensil in between. A food that is fully cooked can become recontaminated from raw foods that contain pathogens.

The way that food is handled after it is contaminated can also make a difference in whether or not an outbreak occurs. Many bacterial microbes need to multiply to a larger number before enough are present in food to cause disease. Given warm moist conditions and an ample supply of nutrients, one bacterium that reproduces by dividing itself every half hour can produce 17 million progeny in 12 hours. As a result, lightly contaminated food left out overnight can be highly infectious by the next day. In general, refrigeration or freezing prevents

animal manure
家畜糞尿
human sewage
生活排水
Salmonella サルモネラ菌
（サルモネラ属の桿菌）

filter feeding shellfish
ろ過摂食性の貝
Vibrio ビブリオ菌
（螺旋菌科ビブリオ属の細菌の総称）

cross contamination
交差汚染（二次汚染）

outbreak
アウトブレイク（予測されるよりも明らかに過剰な疾患の症例が発現すること）

Unit 7   Foodborne Germs and Illness

virtually all bacteria from growing but generally preserves
them in a state of suspended animation. This general rule has
a few surprising exceptions. Two foodborne bacteria, *Listeria
monocytogenes* and *Yersinia enterocolitica* can actually grow at
refrigerator temperatures. High salt, high sugar or high acid
levels keep bacteria from growing, which is why salted meats,
jam, and pickled vegetables are traditional preserved foods.

If food is heated to an internal temperature above 160°F, or
71°C, for even a few seconds, this is sufficient to kill pathogens,
except for the *Clostridium* bacteria, which produce a heat-
resistant form called a spore. *Clostridium* spores are killed only
at temperatures above boiling. This is why canned foods must
be cooked to a high temperature under pressure as part of
the canning process. The toxins produced by bacteria vary in
their sensitivity to heat. The staphylococcal toxin which causes
vomiting is not inactivated even if it is boiled. Fortunately, the
potent toxin that causes botulism is completely inactivated by
boiling.

Foodborne Germs and Illnesses, CDC
https://www.cdc.gov/foodsafety/foodborne-germs.html

suspended animation
仮死状態
Listeria monocytogenes
リステリア・モノサイトゲネ
ス
Yersinia enterocolitica
腸炎エルシニア

Clostridium
クロストリジウム（バチルス科
クロストリジウム属の嫌気性
で芽胞を形成する数種の桿菌
の総称）
spore 芽胞
（一部の細胞が形づくる極め
て耐久性の高い特殊な細胞
構造のこと）

staphylococcal toxin
ブドウ球菌毒素

botulism ボツリヌス中毒

7.1 COMPREHENSION QUESTIONS

Based on the passage, circle either T (true) or F (false) for each of the following statements.

1. *Vibrio* bacteria naturally inhabit coastal waters where oysters live.
   Because oysters feed by filtering water, bacteria can be concentrated.　(T / F)

2. Although many foodborne illnesses are caused by a variety of pathogens,
   there is one "syndrome" that can be described in most cases.　(T / F)

3. When healthy animals are slaughtered, their carcasses can be contaminated
   with the animals' own intestinal contents.　(T / F)

4. All bacteria tend to multiply very rapidly even when in refrigerated
   conditions, forming colonies of millions or even billions of organisms.　(T / F)

5. In the kitchen, poor food handling and manipulation with commonly used,
   contaminated utensils and surfaces can lead to cross contamination with
   microbes.　(T / F)

7.2 PHARMACEUTICAL TERMINOLOGY

医薬品の投与経路に関する接頭辞 (1)

　投与経路に関して最もよく使用される接頭辞にintra- (= within, inside) がある。
Unit 6で扱ったinter-と混同しないように気をつけよう。

● 練習問題

Write the meanings of the word parts and then of the whole given words in Japanese.

1. intradermal
   intra- _____　　dermal _____　　(　　　　　　　　　)

2. intraarterial
   intra- _____　　arterial _____　　(　　　　　　　　　)

3. intravenous
   intra- _____　　venous _____　　(　　　　　　　　　)

4. intramuscular
   intra- _____　　muscular _____　　(　　　　　　　　　)

5. intraperitoneal
   intra- _____　　peritoneal _____　　(　　　　　　　　　)

Unit 7 Foodborne Germs and Illness

7.3 GRAMMAR 「前置詞」

　前置詞は「（名詞の）前に置かれる語」の意味から由来し、「前置詞＋名詞」として前置詞句を形成し、形容詞句や副詞句の働きをする。また、look into, ask forのように特定の動詞と共起して句動詞の形をとるものがあるので、前置詞がどの動詞と共起するかを覚えることが肝要である。

● 練習問題

次の各文の日本語を参考にして、（　）内に適切な前置詞を入れなさい。

1.　細菌は、私たちが好むと好まざるとにかかわらず、私たちの生活において大きな役割をする興味の尽きない微生物である。

   Bacteria are a fascinating type of microorganism that play a large role
   (　　　　　　　　) our lives whether we like it or not.

2.　あなたの細菌サンプルがほんの短時間で繁殖するようすを観察しながら、培養してみなさい。

   Try growing your own sample (　　　　　　　　) bacteria while monitoring
   how it reproduces (　　　　　　) a short space of time.

3.　インフルエンザを予防する最良の方法は、毎年ワクチンを接種することである。

   The best way to prevent the flu is (　　　　　　　) getting vaccinated every
   year.

4.　車は窓を閉めて走っているときのほうが燃料効率は良いでしょうか？

   Is a car more fuel-efficient when traveling (　　　　　　　) the windows up?

5.　私たちにとって幸いなことに、私たちの免疫系は、通常、細菌を無害なものにする。

   Thankfully (　　　　　　　) us, our immune system usually makes bacteria
   harmless.

47

7.4 LISTENING & SPEAKING

Listen to the following conversation and fill in the blanks based on the Japanese.

In a seminar room.

Yuria: In Australia, 1. _____?
(どうしたら薬剤師になれるのですか)

Sophia: First, you must enter a pharmacy program at a university and earn a Bachelor of Pharmacy degree. Then, 2. _____
_____
(卒業生はオーストラリア薬局委員会に登録する必要があります)
and complete an internship of approximately one year.

Yuria: How long is the pharmacy program at university?

Sophia: Usually four years. In Australia, many programs give you a Bachelor's degree if you go to school for three years, 3. _____
_____.
(しかし薬学プログラムでは、4年間の課程を修了しなくてはなりません)

Yuria: In Japan, 4. _____
_____,
(薬剤師になるには大学に6年間通わなくてはなりません)
and we are not paid during our hospital and community pharmacy practices in the fifth year of the program. Do many people go to pharmacy graduate schools in Australia?

Sophia: No. Usually after you finish your studies at a school of pharmacy, you want to work as a pharmacist, at least for a while, to make money. In most cases, the salary you would get as a pharmacist
5. _____
_____.
(博士号をもっているかどうかにかかわらず同額です)
Also, almost no pharmaceutical company has research facilities in Australia, so you would only go back to school to obtain a Ph.D. if you wanted to work in academia.

Unit 7 Foodborne Germs and Illness

7.5 WRITING

次の日本語を英語に訳しなさい。

1. 多くの場合、非競合的拮抗薬は不可逆的に受容体に結合する。

   ヒント 非競合的な：noncompetitive　不可逆的に：irreversibly

   _____

   _____

2. 脂質拡散は、体内での薬物透過にとって最も重要な律速因子である。

   ヒント 拡散：diffusion　透過：permeation　律速因子 limiting factor

   _____

   _____

英語の対応で安心を感じてもらおう

　薬局で日々仕事をしていると、旅行者や留学生など、日本語が話せない患者が薬局を訪れる機会は意外と多い。学生時代から苦手教科だった英語、その苦手意識は今でも変わらない。薬を渡す際、英語で話しかけられただけで、ついつい身構えてしまい、返しの簡単な一言が出てこない。その結果、一方的に薬の使用方法を、片言の英語で伝えて終わりになってしまった。その苦い経験は今でも忘れられない。毎回思うことは、英語がもっと話せれば…という想いである。

　グローバル化が進み、増々英語を必要とする機会は増えていくであろう。その一方で、AI翻訳の発達により、英語ができなくても理解できるようになるかもしれない。だが、人のもつ感性や感情に関しては、コミュニケーションを通じた会話からしか分かり得ない部分があるのでないだろうか。

　あの時、英語をもう少し話すことができていれば、異国の地で、体調を壊し、不安を抱えている患者に少しでも安心を感じてもらうことができたかもしれない。そんな後悔をしないためにも、時間のあるうちに、早い段階で、医療現場で対応できる英語のコミュニケーションスキルを身に着けてほしい。そして、なによりその力が、自分の魅力のひとつになることは間違いないだろう。

萩原裕美

49

Radiation Health Effects

UNIT 8

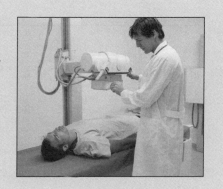

人は呼吸や食品の摂取により、自然界に存在する放射性物質を体内に取り込んでいる。放射線には遺伝子を切断する働きがあるため、身体に浴びると遺伝子が傷つき、障害が生じることがある。しかし、遺伝子には修復能力があり、健康診断での胸部X線のように少量であれば問題はない。どのような場合に放射線は身体に影響を与えるのか見てみよう。

READING

ionizing radiation
電離放射線

Ionizing radiation has sufficient energy to cause chemical changes in cells and damage them. Some cells may die or become abnormal, either temporarily or permanently. By damaging the genetic material (DNA) contained in the body's cells, radiation can cause cancer. Fortunately, our bodies are extremely efficient at repairing cell damage. The extent of the damage to the cells depends upon the amount and duration of the exposure, as well as the organs exposed.

A very large amount of radiation exposure (acute exposure) can cause sickness or even death within hours or days. Such acute exposures are extremely rare.

Chronic Exposure

In general, the amount and duration of radiation exposure affects the severity or type of health effect. There are two broad categories of health effects: chronic (long-term) and acute (short-term).

Chronic exposure is continuous or intermittent exposure to radiation over a long period of time. With chronic exposure, there is a delay between the exposure and the observed health effect. These effects can include cancer and other health outcomes such as benign tumors, cataracts, and potentially harmful genetic changes.

Low Levels of Radiation Exposure

Current science suggests there is some cancer risk from any exposure to radiation. However, it is very hard to tell whether a particular cancer was caused by very low doses of radiation or by something else. The risk of cancer from radiation depends on age, sex, and factors such as tobacco use.

Acute Effects

Acute health effects occur when large parts of the body are exposed to a large amount of radiation. The large exposure can occur all at once or from multiple exposures in a short period of time. Instances of acute effects from environmental sources are very rare. Examples include accidentally handling a strong industrial radiation source or extreme events like nuclear explosions.

It takes a large radiation exposure—more than 75 rad—in a short amount of time to cause acute health effects like radiation sickness. (This level of radiation would be equivalent to an x-ray dose of 75,000 millirem. For comparison, the average dose from an adult chest x-ray is about 4 millirem.)

Exposures between 5 and 10 rad usually result in no acute health effects. However, exposures in this range slightly increase the risk of getting cancer in the future.

---

intermittent 断続的な

cataract 白内障

dose 線量

rad ラド
（吸収した放射線の総量の単位）
radiation sickness
放射線宿酔（放射線照射の直後あるいは数時間後に現れる一過性の全身反応で、吐き気や嘔吐などの胃腸症状、頻脈や血圧低下などの循環器症状、頭痛や眩暈、不安感などの精神神経症状が見られる）
millirem ミリレム
（生物体における放射性粒子の吸収線量の単位）

Exposure Pathways

Understanding the type of radiation received (alpha, beta, gamma, x-ray), the way a person is exposed (external vs. internal), and for how long a person is exposed are all important in estimating health effects.

The risk from exposure to a particular radioactive element depends on:

- The energy of the radiation it emits.

- Its activity (how often it emits radiation).

- The rate at which the body metabolizes and eliminates the radionuclide following ingestion or inhalation.

- Where the radionuclide concentrates in the body and how long it stays there.

The risk that exposure to a radioactive element will cause a particular health effect also depends on whether exposure is internal or external.

- Internal exposure is when radioactive material gets inside the body by eating, drinking, breathing or injection (from certain medical procedures). Alpha and beta particles pose a serious health threat if significant quantities are inhaled or ingested.

- External exposure is when the radioactive source is outside of your body. X-rays and gamma rays can pass through your body, depositing energy as they go.

"Radiation Health Effects," EPA (United States Environmental Protection Agency) website, https://www.epa.gov/radiation/radiation-health-effects

---

activity
壊変速度、放射性崩壊の速さ、放射能

radionuclide
放射性核種（自然に放射線を放出して崩壊し、他の原子核に変わる原子核）

Unit 8　Radiation Health Effects

8.1 COMPREHENSION QUESTIONS

Answer the following questions in English.

1. What factors does the degree of the damage to the cells by radiation depend on?

   _____

2. What health effects can be observed when a person is continuously exposed to radiation?

   _____

3. What situations are some examples of acute exposure to radiation?

   _____

4. Does an x-ray dose of 7 rad immediately affect the body?

   _____

5. What is internal exposure?

   _____

8.2 PHARMACEUTICAL TERMINOLOGY

医薬品の投与経路に関する接頭辞 (2)

　投与経路に関して使われる接頭辞にはintra-の他に、per- (= through)、sub- (= under)、par(a)- (= near) などがある。

● 練習問題

Write the meanings of the word parts and then of the whole given words in Japanese.

1. pernasal

   per- _____　　　nasal _____　　　(　　　　　)

2. percutaneous

   per- _____　　　cutaneous _____　　　(　　　　　)

3. sublingual

   sub- _____　　　lingual _____　　　(　　　　　)

4. subcutaneous

   sub- _____　　　cutaneous _____　　　(　　　　　)

5. parenteral

   para- _____　　　enteral _____　　　(　　　　　)

53

8.3 GRAMMAR 「助動詞」

　助動詞は、「動詞を助ける語」とあるように動詞の前に置かれ、動詞に「可能、義務、意思、許可」などの意味を加える働きをする。

練習問題

次の各文の（　）内に適切な助動詞を入れて、全文を日本語に訳しなさい。

1. A British family is traveling overseas with children when one of them whispers to her mom that she *really, really, REALLY* (　　　　　　) to use the washroom.

   _____

   _____

2. More U.S. teens now vape from electronic cigarettes than smoke conventional tobacco cigarettes. They (　　　　　) think the high-tech devices yield a safe kick from nicotine.

   _____

   _____

3. I (　　　　　) say definitively, that no teenager (　　　　　) be using any tobacco or nicotine-containing products.

   _____

   _____

4. Is it a cold, flu, or allergies? It (　　　　　) be hard to tell them apart because they share so many symptoms.

   _____

   _____

5. These childhood diseases (　　　　　) be dreaded problems that would kill or paralyze children, but now they are not.

   _____

   _____

54

Unit 8 Radiation Health Effects

8.4 LISTENING & SPEAKING

 1-17

Listen to the following conversation and fill in the blanks based on the Japanese.

In a lecture room.

Prof. Miller: Welcome to the class, everyone! 1. _____!
(今日はシンガポールからの特別なゲストスピーカーをお迎えする)

Students: Wow!

Prof. Miller: Do you know anything about Singapore? 2. _____?
(シンガポールの薬剤師について何か知っている人はいるかな)

Marina: I only know that Singapore is a beautiful and advanced country. I've also heard that Singapore is remarkably culturally diverse with Chinese, Malays, and Indians.

Prof. Miller: You're absolutely right!

Shunsuke: Well, talking about pharmacy, 3. _____, but not really about pharmacists in
(アメリカの薬剤師についてはたくさん聞いたことがあります)
Asian countries like Singapore. I'm so curious!

Prof. Miller: Great points, everyone! Why don't we meet our special guest today and 4. _____!
Are you ready?   (シンガポールの薬局業務について学ぼう)

Students: Yes!

Prof. Miller: Please welcome Dr. Regina Chang from the National University of Singapore!

Dr. Chang: Hello everyone! My name is Dr. Regina Chang. I'm from NUS. 5. _____, Prof. Miller.
(すばらしいご紹介をありがとうございます)
Today, I am pleased to have the opportunity to talk about pharmacy practice in Singapore.

55

8.5 WRITING

次の日本語を英語に訳しなさい。

1. 自律神経系は、交感神経系と副交感神経系という2つの系に分けることができる。

   ヒント 自律神経系：autonomic nervous system　交感の：sympathetic
   副交感の：parasympathetic

2. 神経伝達物質の作用を模倣または遮断する薬物を用いることにより、私たちは神経機能を変化させることができる。

   ヒント 模倣する：mimic　遮断する：block　神経機能：neural function

世界に飛び込もう

　国立国際医療研究センター病院で感染症に強い薬剤師を目指してレジデントとして研修をしている。今後、感染症に関わる国際医療支援に携わりたいと考えているが、そのきっかけの一つは学生時代にバックパッカーとして旅をして世界の公衆衛生の現状を見たことだ。

　単に世界を自分の目で見たいというのが始まりだったが、途上国や某自称独立国家などを訪れ、「俺、薬学生だから」という謎の思いつきで、アポなしで病院や薬局、大学を見学させてもらい現実を目の当たりにした。ちなみに、エチオピアでは患者として病院にもかかった。

　ここまで読むと英語ができそうに聞こえるが割と苦手だ。準備はスマホに辞書を入れただけだったが、その場その場で学びながらどうにかやってきた。それでも簡単な単語だけで友人ができた事もあれば、伝わらず危ない目にあった事やジブチの僻地で偶然一緒に食事をしたイタリア人に英語のできなさを説教された夜もあった。

　とりあえず実践してみる事がさらなる取組の原動力になると思う。航空券はスマホで簡単に取れ、飛行機に乗れば地球の裏側でも割とすぐに行ける。行かない理由や行動しない理由を探すより、一度世界に飛び込んでみることをお勧めする。そこから見えてくるものがきっとあると思う。

小泉龍士

Parkinson's Disease

UNIT 9

　パーキンソン病は、1817年に英国のジェームズ・パーキンソン博士によって報告されてから、現在もなお根治が難しく、明白な原因も不明な難病である。米国の有名俳優、マイケル・J・フォックスは1998年にパーキンソン病を公表し、研究や治療に役立てようと研究財団を設立している。米国の国立環境衛生科学研究所を中心に、多くの研究が行われており、近い将来の解明が期待される。

READING

 2-01

What is Parkinson's Disease?

　Parkinson's disease is a progressive neurodegenerative disease, the second most common disorder of this type after Alzheimer's disease. It progresses slowly as small
5　clusters of dopaminergic neurons in the midbrain die. The gradual loss of these neurons results in reduction of a critical neurotransmitter called dopamine, a chemical responsible for transmitting messages to parts of the brain that coordinate muscle movement.

10　Studies have shown that the symptoms of Parkinson's usually appear when 50 percent or more of the dopamine neurons in the midbrain have been lost. Symptoms begin gradually and typically worsen over time.

neurodegenerative
神経変性の

dopaminergic neuron
ドパミン作動性神経細胞

How many people are affected by Parkinson's Disease?

15　It is difficult to know exactly how many people have

Parkinson's disease, since there is no national registry, but it is estimated that at least 500,000 people in the U.S. currently have the disease. The average age of onset is about 60, and prevalence is increasing as the population ages.

The majority of people diagnosed have late-onset sporadic Parkinson's, which does not have a clear genetic cause. About 10 percent have early-onset Parkinson's that often begins before the age of 50. There may be a genetic cause associated with many of these patients. Parkinson's strikes people of all races, ethnic groups, nationalities, and income levels. Actor Michael J. Fox, singer Linda Ronstadt, former U.S. Attorney General Janet Reno, and boxer Muhammad Ali, are among the celebrities living with Parkinson's.

What causes Parkinson's Disease?

The exact cause of Parkinson's disease is unknown. Most researchers agree that the disease is caused by both genetic and environmental factors, and by interactions among these factors.

A full understanding of Parkinson's risk requires integrated efforts to study both genetic and environmental factors. If environmental exposures can be identified, it may lead to new targets for prevention and intervention.

What are the symptoms of Parkinson's Disease?

Common motor symptoms include:

- Tremors or shaking in hands, arms, legs, jaw, and face
- Rigidity or stiffness of limbs and trunk
- Slowness of movement
- Difficulties with balance, speech, and coordination

There are also nonmotor symptoms which may develop
years before the onset of motor problems. These may include:

- Poor sense of smell

- Constipation

- Depression

- Cognitive impairment

- Fatigue

What is NIEHS doing?

NIEHS plans to take advantage of new tools and
technologies. The ultimate goal is to enhance understanding
of the brain and improve prevention, diagnosis, and treatment
of brain diseases, such as Parkinson's disease.

For the past few decades, the development and use of
animal models have provided valuable insight into the
classical motor symptoms of Parkinson's. These models
will continue to shed new light on the pathophysiology of
Parkinson's. Understanding the mechanisms that account for
the selective loss of dopamine neurons may provide important
clues to explain how Parkinson's develops, so that therapies
can be developed to slow or reverse disease progression. For
example, some researchers are beginning to use stem cells that
can be induced to develop into dopamine neurons, in order
to test new cell-based therapies for central nervous system
disorders such as Parkinson's. Other researchers are using
animal models, such as zebrafish, to look at the role that some
chemicals may play in the brain, and to better understand
how neurodegeneration occurs.

Brain imaging techniques and genome-wide association
studies are providing us with additional insight into the
molecular causes of Parkinson's. Since no one can predict
which paths of study will provide major breakthroughs,

NIEHS will continue to support diverse research, involving   75
experts from a wide range of disciplines.

The National Institute of Environmental Health Sciences (NIEHS),
Parkinson's Disease (https://www.niehs.nih.gov/health/topics/
conditions/parkinson/index.cfm)

9.1 COMPREHENSION QUESTIONS

Based on the passage, circle either T (true) or F (false) for each of the following statements.

1. Parkinson's disease is curable.   (T / F)

2. Most Parkinson's patients are diagnosed at a later age with no apparent
    genetic cause.   (T / F)

3. Having constipation or an impaired sense of smell could be a sign of the
    onset of Parkinson's disease.   (T / F)

Answer the following question in English.

What new types of research and technologies have started to enhance our
understanding of Parkinson's disease?

_____

9.2 PHARMACEUTICAL TERMINOLOGY

一般用語と専門用語

　日本語でもそうであるが、医学・薬学英語には、主に医療者間で使用する専門用語
と、患者などに対して使用する一般用語を持つものがある。例えば、analgesic（鎮痛
剤）に対して、painkiller（痛み止め）などである。

● 練習問題

*Match each of the technical terms with the general English term below and then translate
them into Japanese.*

1. antipyretic   (   ) _____   4. ophthalmic solution (   ) _____

2. antitussive   (   ) _____   5. antipruritic   (   ) _____

3. anticoagulant   (   ) _____

(a) anti-itch medication		**(d)** eye drops	
(b) blood thinner		**(e)** fever reducer	
(c) cough medicine			

60

Unit 9　Parkinson's Disease

9.3 GRAMMAR 「関係代名詞」

　　関係代名詞の「関係」とは、文と文を結ぶ接続詞の働きを意味し、「代名詞」は関係代名詞が導く文中での役割をいう。したがって関係代名詞は、文の主語、補語、目的語、あるいは前置詞の目的語などになり得る。

練習問題

次の各文の誤りを正し、全文を日本語に訳しなさい。

1. Don't take prescription medications of which your health care provider has not prescribed for you.

2. Get a flu vaccine each year as early as possible, before or even during flu season, it usually lasts from October to as late as May.

3. The researchers continue to study the children to pinpoint the factors they might reduce asthma risk.

4. There are many kinds of cold medicine. They are different in dosage forms and are dosed according to who's been tested.

5. Most often the gene changes are inherited, but in some cases the changes happen before birth in people their parents don't have them.

61

9.4 LISTENING & SPEAKING 2-02

Listen to the following conversation and fill in the blanks based on the Japanese.

In a lecture room.

Dr. Chang: First of all, I'd like to talk about my homeland. Singapore has become a flourishing country in trade, business, and tourism in recent years. The country has a population of about five million, and about 75% of the population is of Chinese descent, followed by Malays, Indians, and Eurasians. English is the most common language used.

Masayuki: That sounds interesting. Then, how can students become pharmacists?

Dr. Chang: You need to enter NUS, the National University of Singapore. 1. _____.
(これが国内で唯一の薬学部なのです)

Masayuki: Just… one?!

Dr. Chang: Yes. It offers a four-year course culminating in a Bachelor of Science (Pharmacy). 2. _____ _____ and a Residency Training Program.
(Pharm.D.などの専門的な大学院プログラムもあります)

Yuria: What do they do after graduation to get registered as pharmacists? Do they fill prescriptions… like in Japan?

Dr. Chang: 3. _____,
(薬剤師の半数以上が臨床現場で働いています)
and others choose to work at regulatory, research, or pharmaceutical companies.

Yuria: 4. _____.
(それは日本とよく似ているようです)

Dr. Chang: There are many pharmacy technicians supporting the pharmaceutical services in the pharmacy. That enables the pharmacists to participate in patient care by providing their professional pharmaceutical care services and their specialties.

Shunsuke: Pharmacy technicians! I've heard many other countries such as the UK and US have that system. They fill prescriptions, right?

Dr. Chang: Yes. Pharmacists in Singapore are working very hard to contribute to

Unit 9 Parkinson's Disease

the diversifying healthcare needs every day. I think it is the same in Japan, too. We wish to ^{5.} _____

_____! Good luck, everyone!

（よりよい患者ケアのために意見交換してがんばる）

Students: Thank you very much!

9.5 WRITING

次の日本語を英語に訳しなさい。

1. 選択的セロトニン再取り込み阻害薬 (SSRI) が導入された1990年代まで、三環系抗うつ薬 (TCA) は抗うつ薬の主要なクラスであった。

   ヒント 選択的セロトニン再取り込み阻害薬：selective serotonin reuptake inhibitor
   三環系抗うつ薬：tricyclic antidepressant　主要なクラス：dominant class

   _____

   _____

2. プロポフォールは広く使用されている全身静脈麻酔薬だが、鎮痛作用はない。

   ヒント プロポフォール：propofol　全身静脈麻酔薬：intravenous general anesthetic
   鎮痛作用 analgesic property

   _____

   _____

製薬、医療機器企業における英語の必要性

　4年制の薬学部を卒業し、外資の製薬MRとして7年間勤務した。学生時代から英語は得意ではなく、企業に入っても論文を少し読むだけで、英語に触れる機会は殆どなかった。ところが4年前にMRから医療機器の品質部門に異動したことで、少しずつ状況が変化していく。多くの医療機器が海外で製造されているため、英語での報告が基本になっていく。時間があれば、決まった言い回しや過去の報告書を参考にできるため問題はないが、すぐに対応しなければならない時は、困ってしまう。また、海外との電話会議や内部監査に対応する場合は、話されている内容がわからない・言いたいことがすぐに伝えられない場面に出くわし、非常に情けなくなる。現在も新たな仕事内容を担当しているが、資料やトレーニングが全て英語である。英語が使えるだけで仕事ができるわけではないが、自分が持っている有益な専門知識を相手に伝える時に、英語はとても重要なコミュニケーションツールとなっている。そのため、外資系企業で向上心を持って、興味深い仕事やチャンスを実現していくためには、英語スキルは必須である。学生時代に英語学習、特にリスニングやスピーキングに積極的に取り組むことをお勧めする。

千代田尚己

Rheumatoid Arthritis

UNIT 10

関節リウマチは、関節を包む滑膜に炎症が起き、進行すると骨や軟骨が破壊される自己免疫疾患である。関節の痛みや変形を伴い、ひどくなると日常生活に支障をきたす。女性に多くみられ、30代から50代での発症が多い。治療は、ここ十数年で劇的な進歩を遂げており、新薬の開発によるところが大きい。

READING

Rheumatoid arthritis (RA) is an inflammatory disease that causes pain, swelling, stiffness, and loss of function in the joints. It occurs when the immune system, which normally defends the body from invading organisms, turns its attack against the membrane lining the joints.

RA has several features that make it different from other kinds of arthritis. For example, RA generally occurs in a symmetrical pattern. The disease often affects the wrist joints and the finger joints closest to the hand. In addition, people with RA may have fatigue, occasional fevers, and a loss of energy. In most cases RA is chronic, often lifetime.

Who Has RA?

Scientists estimate that about 1.5 million people, or about 0.6 percent of the U.S. adult population, have RA. RA occurs in all races and ethnic groups. The disease occurs much more frequently in women than in men. About two to three times as many women as men have the disease.

line　内側を覆う

What Happens in RA? (See the diagram)

RA is primarily a disease
of the joints where two or
more bones come together.
The ends of the bones are
covered by cartilage, and
the joint is surrounded by
a capsule. The joint capsule
is lined with a type of
tissue called synovium,
which produces synovial
fluid, a clear substance that
lubricates and nourishes
the cartilage and bones
inside the joint capsule.

RA is an autoimmune
disease. Immune cells
attack the synovium and
cause inflammation (synovitis), characterized by warmth,
redness, swelling, and pain. During the inflammation process,
the normally thin synovium becomes thick and makes the
joint swollen, puffy, and sometimes warm to the touch. As RA
progresses, the inflamed synovium invades and destroys the
cartilage and bone within the joint.

Normal Joint

Muscle · Cartilage · Tendon · Synovium · Bone · Synovial Fluid · Bone · Joint Capsule

Joint Affected by Rheumatoid Arthritis — Bone Loss/Erosion · Cartilage Loss · Bone Loss (Generalized) · Inflamed Synovium · Swolled Joint Capsule

Diagram: How RA affects a joint

tendon　腱

cartilage　軟骨

capsule　被膜
joint capsule
関節包、関節被膜

synovium　滑膜

synovial fluid　滑液

lubricate　滑りやすくする

synovitis　滑膜炎
warmth　熱感
redness　発赤
swelling　腫脹

puffy　腫れて柔らかい

What Causes RA?

Scientists still do not know exactly what causes the
immune system to turn against the body's own tissues in
RA, but research has begun to piece together the genetic and
environmental factors involved.

Some scientists also think that a variety of hormonal factors
may be involved. Women are more likely to develop RA

turn against　敵対する

piece together
（情報などの断片をつない
で）全貌を知る

flare 再発する、再び悪化する
contraceptive use 経口避妊薬の使用

than men. The disease may improve during pregnancy and flare after pregnancy. Breastfeeding may also aggravate the disease. Contraceptive use may increase a person's likelihood of developing RA.

How Is RA Treated?

Doctors use a variety of approaches to treat RA, including lifestyle changes, medications and surgery. These are used in different combinations and at different times during the course of the disease and are chosen according to the patient's individual situation.

Medications

analgesic 鎮痛薬
nonsteroidal anti-inflammatory drug 非ステロイド性抗炎症薬
disease-modifying antirheumatic drug 疾患修飾性抗リウマチ薬
hydroxychloroquine ヒドロキシクロロキン
leflunomide レフルノミド
methotrexate メトトレキサート
sulfasalazine スルファサラジン
biologic response modifier 生物学的応答調節剤
cascade カスケード
abatacept アバタセプト
adalimumab アダリムマブ
anakinra アナキンラ
certolizumab セルトリズマブ
etanercept エタネルセプト
golimumab ゴリムマブ
infliximab インフリキシマブ
rituximab リツキシマブ
tocilizumab トシリズマブ
tofacitinib トファシチニブ
Janus kinase ヤーヌスキナーゼ（チロシンキナーゼの1種）
inhibitor 阻害剤

Most people who have RA take medications. Some medications (analgesics) are used only for pain relief; others, such as corticosteroids and nonsteroidal anti-inflammatory drugs (NSAIDs), are used to reduce inflammation. Still others, often called disease-modifying antirheumatic drugs (DMARDs), are used to try to slow the course of the disease. Common DMARDs include hydroxychloroquine, leflunomide, methotrexate, and sulfasalazine.

Other DMARDs—called biologic response modifiers—may be used in people with more serious disease. These are genetically engineered medications that help reduce inflammation and structural damage to the joints by interrupting the cascade of events in inflammation. Currently, several biologic response modifiers are approved for RA, including abatacept, adalimumab, anakinra, certolizumab, etanercept, golimumab, infliximab, rituximab, and tocilizumab. Another DMARD, tofacitinib, from a new class of drugs called Janus kinase (JAK) inhibitors, fights inflammation from inside the cell to reduce inflammation in people with RA.

Extracted from: National Institute of Arthritis and Musculoskeletal and Skin Diseases, Handout on Health: Rheumatoid Arthritis https://www.niams.nih.gov/health_Info/Rheumatic_Disease/default.asp#ra_3

Unit 10 Rheumatoid Arthritis

⑩.1 COMPREHENSION QUESTIONS

Answer the following questions in English.

1. Explain the sentence "RA generally occurs in a symmetrical pattern" in paragraph 2. What does it mean?

   _____

2. What are the four classical signs of inflammation?

   _____

3. Describe the mechanism of how the attack by the immune cells leads to the destruction of the bone in rheumatoid arthritis.

   _____

4. What are the risk factors for rheumatoid arthritis?

   _____

5. What does NSAIDs stand for?

   _____

⑩.2 PHARMACEUTICAL TERMINOLOGY

処方箋の略語 (1)

　英語の処方箋に使われる略語は、ラテン語に由来するものが多い。
d (*die*) = day、h (*hora*) = hourなどがある。

● 練習問題

Match each of the following abbreviations with its meaning below.

1. s.i.d. (*semel in die*)　　(　)　　4. q.i.d. (*quater in die*)　　(　)

2. b.i.d. (*bis in die*)　　(　)　　5. q.4h. (*quaque 4 hora*)　　(　)

3. t.i.d. (*ter in die*)　　(　)

(a) every four hours	**(d)** three times a day
(b) four times a day	**(e)** twice a day
(c) once a day	

67

10.3 GRAMMAR 「基本五文型」

英語は、文の構成要素（主語、動詞、目的語、補語）の並べ方によって、5つの基本文型に分けられる。

(1) S＋V（「〜は…する」）

(2) S＋V＋C（「〜は…である〔になる〕」）　〔S＝C〕

(3) S＋V＋O（「〜は－を…する」）　〔S ≠ O〕

(4) S＋V＋O＋O（「〜は－に－を…する」）

(5) S＋V＋O＋C（「〜は－を〔が〕－と〔に〕…する」）　〔O＝C〕

練習問題

次の各文は何文型かを考え、全文を日本語に訳しなさい。

1. Grapefruit juice does not affect all the drugs.〔第＿＿文型〕

　　_____

2. Grapefruit juice and the actual grapefruit can be part of a healthy diet.

〔第＿＿文型〕

　　_____

3. The severity of the interaction can be different depending on the person, the drug, and the amount of grapefruit juice you drink.〔第＿＿文型〕

　　_____

　　_____

4. Many drugs are broken down (metabolized) with the help of a vital enzyme called CYP3A4 in the small intestine.〔第＿＿文型〕

　　_____

　　_____

5. Scientists have known for several decades that grapefruit juice can affect the absorption of certain drugs in the body.〔第＿＿文型〕

　　_____

　　_____

Unit 10   Rheumatoid Arthritis

10.4 LISTENING & SPEAKING 2-04

Listen to the following conversation and fill in the blanks based on the Japanese.

At a pharmacy.

Student Pharmacist: Good morning, my name is Haruna Goto and 1. _____

_____.

（私は薬学生で、今日はあなたのお手伝いをします）

Patient: Hello. I need this prescription filled.

Student Pharmacist: May I have your name and your prescription?

Patient: My name is Jimmy Bradshaw and here is my prescription.

Student Pharmacist: Thank you, Mr. Bradshaw. 2. _____

_____.

（お座りください。処方箋の調剤ができましたらお呼びします）

Patient: Thank you.

Student Pharmacist: Mr. Bradshaw?

Patient: Yes.

Student Pharmacist: 3. _____.

（処方箋の準備ができました）

Oh, before I forget, do you have any allergies?

Patient: No, I don't.

Student Pharmacist: I see. You have just one medicine today. 4. _____

_____.

（食後に一日3回、カプセルを一度に2つお飲みください）

Be sure to take these with a large glass of water.

Patient: I will be sure to do so.

Student Pharmacist: Do you have any questions?

Patient: No. Thank you for asking.

Student Pharmacist: Not at all. 5. _____!

（すばらしい一日を。お大事に）

69

10.5 WRITING

次の日本語を英語に訳しなさい。

1. 非ステロイド性抗炎症薬（NSAID）の抗炎症作用は、プロスタグランジン生合成の阻害によって引き起こされる。

   ヒント プロスタグランジン生合成：prostaglandin biosynthesis

   _____

   _____

2. がん治療のために、従来の化学療法に加えて、チェックポイント阻害剤療法と呼ばれる新たな免疫療法が今では受けられる。

   ヒント 免疫療法：immunotherapy

   _____

   _____

英語はBODY LANGUAGEでいい!?

　私が米国の州立大学の学生だった1980年代、LINEはもちろんメールもインターネットもなかった。電話はバカ高い。「エアメール」封筒が届くのがどれだけ楽しみだったか。

　日本で地方の公立高校を卒業したばかりの私は英語が得意ではなかった。元来の理系女、入学当初は数学、生物、化学など内容がわかるクラスを選択する作戦に出た。英語力が必要なクラスは後回しに。当時も大学には世界中の留学生がいた。二世三世の東洋人も沢山住んでいた。私の名前や顔だけでは最近きたばかりの英語がタドタドしい外国人とはわからないし、評価に留学生優遇措置は一切ない厳しさだった。

　卒業後は日本国内でいくつかの仕事に就いた。外資系製薬会社では学術情報やマーケティングの仕事。他国とのやり取りも多く英語は必須。身につけた英語で世界相手に仕事ができた。今でも英字新聞の理解は難しいが医科学系文書は理解できる。つまり、世界中の医師や薬剤師と共通の会話ができる。

　現在、皆さんの周りには英語があふれている。私の時代とは大違い。ためらうことなく英語の海へ飛び込んでほしい。そこに手を、顔を、声をだして！　皆さんにとって得るものしかないはず。英語はbody languageはダメ！　ちゃんとした英語で可能性を広げて欲しい。

高橋香織

Heart Disease

UNIT 11

心臓の病気は日本人の死因ではがんに次いで第2位である。心臓病にならないためにはリスクを高める高血圧や高コレステロール、糖尿病、肥満などを予防することが大切である。しかし万一発症した場合には、初期症状を見逃すことなく早期に治療を開始することで健康な生活を送ることができる。多くの人が無視してしまいがちな心臓病の軽い前兆症状とはどのようなものであろうか。

● READING

 2-05

What Is Coronary Heart Disease?

Coronary heart disease (CHD) is a disease in which a waxy substance called plaque builds up inside the coronary arteries. These arteries supply oxygen-rich blood to your heart muscle.
5 When plaque builds up in the arteries, the condition is called atherosclerosis. The buildup of plaque occurs over many years.

Over time, plaque can harden or rupture. Hardened plaque narrows the coronary arteries and reduces the flow of oxygen-rich blood to the heart. If the plaque ruptures, a blood clot
10 can form on its surface. A large blood clot can mostly or completely block blood flow through a coronary artery. Over time, ruptured plaque also hardens and narrows the coronary arteries.

coronary heart disease
冠(状)動脈性心疾患
plaque プラーク、斑点

atherosclerosis
アテローム性動脈硬化症

blood clot 血栓

71

angina 狭心症

silent CHD
無症候性CHD
heart attack 心臓発作

heart failure 心不全
arrhythmia 不整脈

platelet
血小板

scar tissue
はんこん
瘢痕組織

fullness
膨満感

What Are Signs and Symptoms of Coronary Heart Disease?

A common symptom of CHD is angina. Angina is chest 15
pain or discomfort that occurs if an area of your heart muscle
doesn't get enough oxygen-rich blood. Angina may feel like
pressure or squeezing in your chest. You also may feel it in
your shoulders, arms, neck, jaw, or back. Angina pain may
even feel like indigestion. The pain tends to get worse with 20
activity and go away with rest. Emotional stress can also
trigger the pain.

Some people who have CHD have no signs or symptoms—a
condition called silent CHD. The disease might not be
diagnosed until a person has signs or symptoms of a heart 25
attack, heart failure, or an arrhythmia.

Heart Attack

A heart attack occurs if the flow of oxygen-rich blood to a
section of heart muscle is cut off. This can happen if an area
of plaque in a coronary artery ruptures. Blood cell fragments 30
called platelets stick to the site of the injury and may clump
together to form blood clots. If a clot becomes large enough, it
can mostly or completely block blood flow through a coronary
artery. If the blockage isn't treated quickly, the portion of heart
muscle fed by the artery begins to die. Healthy heart tissue 35
is replaced with scar tissue. The most common heart attack
symptom is chest pain or discomfort. Most heart attacks involve
discomfort in the center or left side of the chest that often lasts
for more than a few minutes or goes away and comes back. The
discomfort can feel like uncomfortable pressure, squeezing, 40
fullness, or pain. The feeling can be mild or severe. Heart
attack pain sometimes feels like indigestion or heartburn. The
symptoms of angina can be similar to the symptoms of a heart
attack. Angina pain usually lasts for only a few minutes and

Unit 11 Heart Disease

goes away with rest. Chest pain or discomfort that doesn't go
away or changes from its usual pattern (for example, occurs
more often or while you're resting) might be a sign of a heart
attack.

Heart Failure

Heart failure is a condition in which your heart can't pump
enough blood to meet your body's needs. Heart failure doesn't
mean that your heart has stopped or is about to stop working.
The most common signs and symptoms of heart failure are
shortness of breath or trouble breathing; fatigue; and swelling
in the ankles, feet, legs, stomach, and veins in the neck. All of
these symptoms are the result of fluid buildup in your body.
When symptoms start, you may feel tired and short of breath
after routine physical effort, like climbing stairs.

Arrhythmia

An arrhythmia is a problem with the rate or rhythm of the
heartbeat. When you have an arrhythmia, you may notice that
your heart is skipping beats or beating too fast. Some people
describe arrhythmias as a fluttering feeling in the chest. These
feelings are called palpitations. Some arrhythmias can cause
your heart to suddenly stop beating. This condition is called
sudden cardiac arrest (SCA). SCA usually causes death if it's
not treated within minutes.

palpitation
動悸、心悸亢進

sudden cardiac arrest
突然心停止

Coronary Heart Disease
https://www.nhlbi.nih.gov/health/health-topics/topics/cad
https://www.nhlbi.nih.gov/health/health-topics/topics/cad/signs

11.1 COMPREHENSION QUESTIONS

Based on the passage, circle either T (true) or F (false) for each of the following statements.

1. A buildup of plaque in the arteries occurs in a few years. (T / F)

2. You may feel angina pain not only in your chest but also in your shoulders, arms, neck, jaws, or back. (T / F)

3. Chest pain or discomfort in a heart attack can feel like indigestion or heartburn. (T / F)

4. In heart failure the heart will stop working. (T / F)

5. An arrhythmia may cause you to have palpitations. (T / F)

11.2 PHARMACEUTICAL TERMINOLOGY

処方箋の略語 (2)

　英語の処方箋によく使われる略語には、a (*ante*) = before、p (*post*) = after、c (*cibo*) = meal、q (*quaque*) = every, each などがある。

　なお、米国の医療系団体 The Joint Commission は手書きの場合などに間違えやすい略語の使用について、"Do Not Use" List*を作って注意を呼び掛けている。例えば、q.d.(= daily）とq.o.d. (= every other day) は混同しやすいので、略語ではなく英単語で記載するよう指導している。

(*https://www.jointcommission.org/facts_about_do_not_use_list/)

● 練習問題

Match each of the following abbreviations with its meaning below.

1. q.d. (*quaque die*) 　　(　　)

2. a.c. (*ante cibos*) 　　(　　)

3. p.c. (*post cibos*) 　　(　　)

4. p.r.n. (*pro re nata*) 　(　　)

5. h.s. (*hora somni*) 　　(　　)

(a) after meals	**(b)** as needed	**(c)** before bed
(d) before meals	**(e)** every day	

74

Unit 11　Heart Disease

11.3 GRAMMAR　「無生物主語」

　　無生物主語は、人や生き物以外の無生物を主語にして、あたかも意思があるかのような表現をいう。無生物主語が原因や理由を表すように訳すと、文意が理解しやすくなる。

● 練習問題

次の各文の下線部に注意して、全文を日本語に訳しなさい。

1.　Some cells <u>allow</u> your body to jump, run, or throw a ball.

2.　Your ears <u>allow</u> you to hear music or your mom calling you for dinner.

3.　Your sense of touch <u>lets</u> you pet a soft kitten or decide if the bathwater is warm enough.

4.　Advances in brain imaging <u>allow</u> us to predict psychotherapy success in patients with social anxiety disorder.

5.　A hormone called insulin <u>allows</u> glucose to enter all the cells of your body and be used as energy.

75

11.4 LISTENING & SPEAKING

 2-06

Listen to the following conversation and fill in the blanks based on the Japanese.

At a pharmacy.

Patient: Excuse me, do you speak English?

Student Pharmacist: Oh, hello! Yes, I do. How may I help you?

Patient: This is my first time here and I need a prescription filled. Can you help me?

Student Pharmacist: Sure. But as this is your first time here, 1. _____

_____?

(患者さん用の質問票にご記入いただけますか)

Patient: Is it in English?

Student Pharmacist: Yes, it is. Here you go and here is a pen. Please have a seat and

2. _____.

(終わりましたらこちらにお渡しください)

Patient: Here you are. I am finished.

Student Pharmacist: Thank you so much, Mr. Johnson. My name is Sarina and I am a student pharmacist. I will be helping you today. Your name is Michael Johnson?

Patient: Yes, it is.

Student Pharmacist: 3. _____

_____?

(そしてこちらが現在のご住所とお電話番号ですね)

Patient: Yes, they are.

Student Pharmacist: Great! I understand everything and will now fill your prescription after I enter you into our database. Please have a seat and I will get back to you.

Patient: Thank you so much. 4. _____

_____?

(ところで、これは20分以上かかりますか)

Student Pharmacist: I don't think so. We aren't so busy, 5. _____

_____.

(ですから、10分ほどで戻れるはずです)

Unit 11　Heart Disease

11.5 WRITING

次の日本語を英語に訳しなさい。

1. 狭心症は虚血性心疾患の最も一般的な徴候であり、それに対しては血管拡張薬が有効である。

   ヒント　狭心症：angina pectoris　虚血性の：ischemic　徴候：sign
   血管拡張薬：vasodilator

   _____

   _____

2. エピネフリン（アドレナリン）は、非常に強力な血管収縮薬および強心薬である。

   ヒント　強力な：potent　血管収縮薬：vasoconstrictor　強心薬：cardiac stimulant

   _____

   _____

国際社会における薬剤師の役割

　近年、日本ではグローバル人材育成が課題となっている。語学力やコミュニケーション力が高い人材を思い浮かべるかもしれないが、強みはそれだけではない。主体的かつ積極的に物事に取り組む能力、チャレンジ精神、異文化理解と柔軟な対応能力、多様な人々との協調性など幅広い。海外生活において様々な困難に遭遇する中で日本人としてのアイデンティティを意識するようになるとともに、国際的視野が養われていく。

　留学をしなくても、英語のコミュニケーション力を磨き、国際交流イベントや海外ボランティアへの参加など、海外の人々との触れ合いを通じて異文化理解を深めることができる。国内の学会でも国際シンポジウムを設ける学会が増えてきている。学生でも薬剤師でも、国内外での国際交流に積極的に関わる姿勢があれば国際的視野を培うことが可能である。

　海外情報を得るだけでなく、世界に向けた情報発信を行い、世界の医療に貢献していく必要がある。例えば、自然災害や高齢化社会への対応などは海外の医療人が特に情報を必要としている領域で、日本には十分な経験がある。日本の経験を世界で役立ててもらえるように、国際学会・シンポジウムに参加し、発表し、国際雑誌への論文投稿も目指していこう！

　　　　　　　　　　　　　　　　　　　　　　　　　　　　　　岩澤真紀子

What Is COPD

UNIT 12

COPD（慢性閉塞性肺疾患）とは、喫煙や大気中の有害物質などの影響で呼吸器に炎症が生じ、不可逆的に呼吸が障害される疾患である。WHOの統計によると、2015年に世界全体で320万人の命を奪って死亡原因の第4位を占め、2020年には第3位になると予想されている。この病気にはどのような治療法があるのか、現状を見てみよう。

READING

 2-07

COPD, or chronic obstructive pulmonary disease, is a progressive disease that makes it hard to breathe. Progressive means the disease gets worse over time. COPD can cause coughing that produces large amounts of a slimy substance called mucus, wheezing, shortness of breath, chest tightness, and other symptoms.

COPD has no cure yet. However, lifestyle changes and treatments can help you feel better, stay more active, and slow the progress of the disease.

Lifestyle Changes

Quit Smoking and Avoid Lung Irritants

Quitting smoking is the most important step you can take to treat COPD. Talk with your doctor about programs and products that can help you quit. Also, try to avoid secondhand smoke and places with dusts, fumes, or other toxic substances that you may inhale.

---

wheezing
喘鳴（呼吸時にヒューヒュー、ゼーゼーと音がすること）
shortness of breath
息切れ
chest tightness
胸部絞扼感（胸がしめつけられる感覚）

secondhand smoke
二次喫煙（喫煙者の吐き出した煙や火のついたタバコから生じる煙を吸い込むこと）
fume
煙気（悪臭や有害性のあるガスや蒸気）

Medicines

Bronchodilators

Bronchodilators relax the muscles around your airways.
20 This helps open your airways and makes breathing easier.

Depending on the severity of your COPD, your doctor
may prescribe short-acting or long-acting bronchodilators.
Short-acting bronchodilators last about 4–6 hours and should
be used only when needed. Long-acting bronchodilators last
25 about 12 hours or more and are used every day.

Most bronchodilators are taken using a device called an
inhaler. This device allows the medicine to go straight to your
lungs. Not all inhalers are used the same way. Ask your health
care providers to show you the correct way to use your inhaler.

30 If your COPD is mild, your doctor may only prescribe a
short-acting inhaled bronchodilator. In this case, you may
use the medicine only when symptoms occur. If your COPD
is moderate or severe, your doctor may prescribe regular
treatment with short- and long-acting bronchodilators.

35 ### *Bronchodilators Plus Inhaled Glucocorticosteroids (Steroids)*

In general, using inhaled steroids alone is not a preferred
treatment. If your COPD is more severe, or if your symptoms
flare up often, your doctor may prescribe a combination of
40 medicines that includes a bronchodilator and an inhaled
steroid. Steroids help reduce airway inflammation.

Your doctor may ask you to try inhaled steroids with the
bronchodilator for a trial period of 6 weeks to 3 months to
see whether the addition of the steroid helps relieve your
45 breathing problems.

---

bronchodilator
気管支拡張薬

inhaler 吸入器

glucocorticosteroid
グルココルチコステロイド

flare up 再燃する

Vaccines

Flu Shots

The flu, or influenza, can cause serious problems for people who have COPD. Flu shots can reduce your risk of getting the flu. Talk with your doctor about getting a yearly flu shot.

Pneumococcal Vaccine

This vaccine lowers your risk for pneumococcal pneumonia and its complications. People who have COPD are at higher risk for pneumonia than people who do not have COPD. Talk with your doctor about whether you should get this vaccine.

Pulmonary Rehabilitation

Pulmonary rehabilitation or rehab is a broad program that helps improve the well-being of people who have chronic breathing problems. Rehab may include an exercise program, disease management training, and nutritional and psychological counseling. The program's goal is to help you stay active and carry out your daily activities.

Oxygen Therapy

If you have severe COPD and low levels of oxygen in your blood, oxygen therapy can help you breathe better. For this treatment, oxygen is delivered through nasal prongs or a mask. You may need extra oxygen all the time or only at certain times. For some people who have severe COPD, using extra oxygen for most of the day can help them.

National Heart, Lung, and Blood Institute, What Is COPD
(https://www.nhlbi.nih.gov/health/health-topics/topics/copd)

---

pneumococcal
肺炎球菌の
pneumonia
肺炎

pulmonary rehabilitation
呼吸リハビリテーション

nasal prong 鼻カニューレ
（酸素吸入用のチューブ）

Unit 12 What Is COPD

12.1 COMPREHENSION QUESTIONS

Answer the following questions in English.

1. What are some of the symptoms of COPD?

   _____

2. How can COPD patients slow the progress of the disease?

   _____

3. When should COPD patients use short-acting bronchodilators?

   _____

4. Why is it important for COPD patients to get flu shots?

   _____

5. How can COPD patients have their blood oxygen levels raised?

   _____

12.2 PHARMACEUTICAL TERMINOLOGY

処方箋の略語 (3)

投与経路を表す略語には、p, P (*per*) = through、I = intra などがある。

● 練習問題

Match each of the following abbreviations with its meaning below and then translate them into Japanese.

1. PO または p.o. (*per os*)　（　　）　_____

2. IM または im　（　　）　_____

3. SQ または SC　（　　）　_____

4. IV または iv　（　　）　_____

5. PR または pr　（　　）　_____

(a) by mouth	**(b)** intramuscular	**(c)** intravenous
(d) per rectum	**(e)** subcutaneous	

81

12.3 GRAMMAR 「仮定法」

　　仮定法とは、「現実には起こらない、起こって欲しくないこと」を言う場合に用いる。現実に起こらないことは過去形、過去に起こらなかったことは過去完了形で表す。as if〜、if only〜、imagine〜、suppose〜などの表現にも仮定法がしばしば使われる。

練習問題

次の各文の下線部に注意して、全文を日本語に訳しなさい。

1.　If your blood <u>didn't</u> clot, you <u>could</u> bleed to death.

2.　For toys to be considered minimal risk, the FDA recommends that the levels of radiation and light <u>not exceed</u> the limits for Class 1.

3.　The FDA has required that some prescription and over-the-counter (OTC) drugs taken by mouth <u>include</u> warnings against drinking grapefruit juice.

4.　The world we live in today would no doubt be a different place if it <u>weren't</u> for the amazing scientific discoveries.

5.　Call your healthcare provider if your child's symptoms do not go away when you <u>would</u> expect them to go away.

82

Unit 12　What Is COPD

12.4 LISTENING & SPEAKING 2-08

Listen to the following conversation and fill in the blanks based on the Japanese.

At a pharmacy.

Student Pharmacist: Mr. Li?

Patient: Yes, that's me.

Student Pharmacist: We have filled your prescription, 1._____

_____. Do you have time?

（ですが、いくつか確認させていただきたい点があります）

Patient: I have to leave in about five minutes, is that OK?

Student Pharmacist: It should be. My name is Mizuki and I'm a student pharmacist. Do you have any allergies to drugs or foods?

Patient: 2._____.

（はい、ペニシリンにアレルギーがあります）

Student Pharmacist: I see. And that is listed in your medical record handbook.

Patient: Yes, it is. It says so right here.

Student Pharmacist: Have you taken this medicine before?

Patient: No, I haven't. Can you tell me how to take it? 3._____

_____?

（それと、知っておくべき注意点はありますか）

Student Pharmacist: Sure. First, be sure to take this 30 minutes after you finish a meal. 4._____.

（空腹時にはそれを服用しないでください）

You will take two pills at a time, three times a day, for one week.

Patient: I see. Is it OK to take this with my other prescription?

Student Pharmacist: Just a second please. Yes, it is. 5._____

_____.

（この2種類の処方箋薬は同時に服用できます）

Patient: I see. Thank you so much. You have been very helpful, Mizuki.

Student Pharmacist: It's my pleasure. And please take care and have a great week.

83

12.5 WRITING

次の日本語を英語に訳しなさい。

1. イソプロテレノールは、喘息の治療のために使われる強力な気管支拡張薬である。

   ヒント イソプロテレノール：isoproterenol　気管支拡張薬：bronchodilator

2. この薬は、加圧容器からミクロエアロゾルとして吸入する。

   ヒント 加圧容器：pressurized canister　ミクロエアロゾル：microaerosol

真摯な対応ができる医療従事者には、教養と語学力が必須

　緩和ケアとは、生命を脅かす疾患による問題に直面している患者とその家族に対して、痛みやその他の身体的問題、心理社会的問題、スピリチュアルな問題を早期に発見し、的確なアセスメントと対処（治療・処置）を行うことによって、苦しみを予防し、和らげることで、クオリティー・オブ・ライフ（QOL：生活の質）を改善するアプローチである。【WHO(世界保健機関)による緩和ケアの定義（2002年）】

　緩和ケアを実践する場合にはどのようなことに気を付ければよいのだろうか。問題を解決するためのアプローチを行うわけだが、患者さんの問題を理解共感しなければ医療従事者としての信頼を得ることができない。患者さんは、今まで私達が困ったことがないようなことに対して苦しみを感じていることがある。患者さんが訴えている痛みは本当に体の痛みだろうか？　評価を誤ってしまうことで本来必要のない薬が処方されてしまうかもしれない。患者さんの生活背景や信仰、文化を理解していくための教養と語学力を身につけることで、患者さんの問題点をより的確に評価する手助けとなる。まずは、自身が死生観を持って、真摯な対応ができる医療従事者を目指してみませんか。

門谷靖裕

Diabetes

UNIT 13

わが国において生活習慣の欧米化などの影響により糖尿病患者数の増加が課題となっている。糖尿病は放置すると様々な合併症や身体の障害が現れる深刻な病気である。糖尿病のうち2型糖尿病は生活習慣病とも言われている。米国においても問題は深刻である。米国における2型糖尿病の状況や予防策を見てみよう。

READING

 2-09

Type 2 Diabetes and Prediabetes

Type 2 diabetes is a disorder that affects the way the body uses digested food for growth and energy. Normally, the food one eats is broken down into glucose, a form of sugar. The
5 glucose then passes into the bloodstream, where it is used by the cells for growth and energy. For glucose to reach the cells, however, insulin must be present. Insulin is a hormone produced by the pancreas, a fist-sized gland behind the stomach.

10 Most people with type 2 diabetes have two problems: insulin resistance—a condition in which muscle, liver, and fat cells do not use insulin properly—and reduced insulin production by the pancreas. As a result, glucose builds up in the blood, overflows into the urine, and passes out of the body,
15 never fulfilling its role as the body's main source of fuel.

About 23.6 million people in the United States have diabetes. Of those, 17.9 million are diagnosed and 5.7 million

prediabetes
前糖尿病、糖尿病前症

insulin resistance
インスリン抵抗性

About 23.6 million people
CDCによる最新の統計では、診断確定2300万人、未診断720万人、計3020万人

85

undiagnosed
未診断の（CDCによると糖尿病であることに気づいていないか、または報告していないこと）
new-onset
新規の（初めて発症すること）

are undiagnosed. Ninety to 95 percent of people with diabetes have type 2 diabetes. Diabetes is the main cause of kidney failure, limb amputation, and new-onset blindness in American adults. People with diabetes are more likely than people without diabetes to develop and die from diseases of the heart and blood vessels, called cardiovascular disease. Adults with diabetes have heart disease death rates about two to four times higher than adults without diabetes, and the risk for stroke is two to four times higher among people with diabetes.

Prediabetes is a condition in which blood glucose levels are higher than normal but not high enough for a diagnosis of diabetes. Prediabetes is also called impaired glucose tolerance (IGT) or impaired fasting glucose (IFG), depending on the test used to measure blood glucose levels. Having prediabetes puts one at higher risk for developing type 2 diabetes. People with prediabetes are also at increased risk for developing cardiovascular disease.

impaired glucose tolerance
耐糖能異常
impaired fasting glucose
空腹時血糖異常

Prediabetes is becoming more common in the United States. The U.S. Department of Health and Human Services estimates that about one in four U.S. adults aged 20 years or older—or 57 million people—had prediabetes in 2007. Those with prediabetes are likely to develop type 2 diabetes within 10 years, unless they take steps to prevent or delay diabetes.

U.S. Department of Health and Human Services
米国保健福祉省

Who should be tested for prediabetes and diabetes?

The American Diabetes Association recommends that testing to detect prediabetes and type 2 diabetes be considered in adults without symptoms who are overweight or obese and have one or more additional risk factors for diabetes. In those without these risk factors, testing should begin at age 45.

Risk factors for prediabetes and diabetes—in addition to

overweight
過体重の（「過体重」はBMIが25以上、「肥満」はBMIが30以上）

Unit 13 Diabetes

being overweight or obese or being age 45 or older—include
the following:

- being physically inactive

- having a parent, brother, or sister with diabetes

- having a family background that is African American,
  Alaska Native, American Indian, Asian American,
  Hispanic/Latino, or Pacific Islander

- giving birth to a baby weighing more than 9 pounds or
  being diagnosed with gestational diabetes—diabetes first
  found during pregnancy

- having high blood pressure—140/90 mmHg or above—or
  being treated for high blood pressure

- having HDL, or "good," cholesterol below 35 mg/dL, or a
  triglyceride level above 250 mg/dL

- having polycystic ovary syndrome, also called PCOS

- having impaired fasting glucose (IFG) or impaired glucose
  tolerance (IGT) on previous testing

- having other conditions associated with insulin resistance,
  such as severe obesity or a condition called acanthosis
  nigricans, characterized by a dark, velvety rash around
  the neck or armpits

- having a history of cardiovascular disease

If results of testing are normal, testing should be repeated
at least every 3 years. Doctors may recommend more frequent
testing depending on initial results and risk status.

https://www.niddk.nih.gov/about-niddk/research-areas/diabetes/
diabetes-prevention-program-dpp/Pages/default.aspx

---

gestational diabetes
妊娠糖尿病

HDL high density
lipoprotein (高密度リポ蛋白)
の略語
triglyceride トリグリセリド
(3つの水酸基の各々が脂肪
酸でエステル化したグリセロ
ール)
**polycystic ovary
syndrome**
多嚢胞性卵巣症候群(卵巣の
硬化性嚢胞性疾患)

acanthosis nigricans
黒色表皮腫
velvety
ビロードのようになめらかな

ⓛ COMPREHENSION QUESTIONS

Based on the passage, circle either T (true) or F (false) for each of the following statements.

1. In the U.S., about one in three diabetic patients are not diagnosed with
   diabetes. (T / F)

2. Diabetes is the leading cause of kidney failure in the U.S. (T / F)

3. Prediabetes is a kind of diabetes which is experienced by young patients.
   (T / F)

4. It is estimated that about 25 percent of the whole population has prediabetes
   in the U.S. (T / F)

5. The American Diabetes Association recommends that people who are
   over 45 take tests for diabetes even if they do not have any risk factors. (T / F)

ⓛ PHARMACEUTICAL TERMINOLOGY

数量単位を表す表現

　ここで取り上げた表現のうち、milli-、centi-、deci-、dec(a)-、hecto-、centi-、kilo-は接頭辞である。体積の単位リットルには記号lとLの2つが併用されている。大文字のLは小文字のlと数字の1の混同を避けるために、1979年国際度量衡総会（CGPM）で暫定的に導入され、そのときの決議で、l とLの使用状況を見ながら、どちらか一方を削除することになっているが、その決着を見ないまま現在に至っている（国立研究開発法人産業技術総合研究所HPより）。

m, milli (= 10^{-3})、centi (= 10^{-2})、d, deci (= 10^{-1})、deca (= 10)、hecto, centi (= 10^2)、k, kilo (= 10^3)、g (= gram)、m (= meter)、L (= liter)

● 練習問題

Write a word for each of the following abbreviations.

（例）mm _____millimeter_____

1. mg _____   4. mL _____

2. kg _____   5. dL _____

3. cm _____

Unit 13 Diabetes

13.3 GRAMMAR 「同格」

同格とは、名詞または名詞相当語句の意味を補ったり、言い換えたりする表現を言う。

● 練習問題

次の各文の同格関係に注意して、全文を日本語に訳しなさい。

1. 2,300 milligrams per day are about roughly one teaspoon of salt, the daily consumption amount recommended in the guidelines.

   _____

   _____

2. If you touch a hot surface, the sensory organs of your fingertips will send the message to your central nervous system that this surface is very hot.

   _____

   _____

3. If you smell good food, your brain reminds you that you're hungry. Saliva, or spit, makes the food soft and gooey.

   _____

   _____

4. There is no question that physiology changes as we age.

   _____

5. Bacteria that cause disease have millions of different genomes, or sequences of genetic code.

   _____

   _____

89

13.4 LISTENING & SPEAKING

 2-10

Listen to the following conversation and fill in the blanks based on the Japanese.

At a pharmacy.

Student Pharmacist: Good afternoon, can I help you?

Patient: 1._____. Can you help me?
(はい、市販薬の解熱剤を探しています)

Student Pharmacist: Sure. My name is Erina and I'm a fifth-year student pharmacist.

Patient: Hello, Erina. My name is Charles.

Student Pharmacist: That's a cool name. 2._____?
(ところで、このお薬はご自分用ですか)

Patient: Actually no. It is for my baby. He is 16 months old.

Student Pharmacist: I see. 3._____?
(熱はどのくらいで、いつ始まったのですか)

Patient: It started this morning and it is not so high: 37 degrees Celsius.

Student Pharmacist: I see. I hope he gets well soon. We have children's Tylenol over here. 4._____.
(私と一緒にいらしてください)

Patient: Thank you so much!

Student Pharmacist: Here you go. This is in a syrup form. It will be easier to give to your child than a pill.

Patient: I see. Thank you so much.

Student Pharmacist: You're welcome. Now please follow me to the cash register.

Patient: Sure. 5._____?
(おいくらになりますか)

Student Pharmacist: This syrup will be 860 yen. That includes consumption tax.

90

Unit 13　Diabetes

13.5 WRITING

次の日本語を英語に訳しなさい。

1. アルコール摂取は薬物代謝にしばしば影響する。

   ヒント　摂取：alcohol intake

   _____

   _____

2. アルコールデヒドロゲナーゼは、アルコールからアセトアルデヒドへの変換を触媒する。

   ヒント　デヒドロゲナーゼ：dehydrogenase　　アセトアルデヒド：acetaldehyde

   _____

   _____

在宅医療について

　在宅医療って知っている？　文字通り、自宅で医療を受けることである。医療法の中に、「居宅」という言葉で在宅医療が認められている。在宅医療を利用するにあたっては、医療機関に通院できない患者さんが対象になる。我が国では、高齢者が増えてきていることがその背景にある。在宅医療は医療の提供だけではなく、生活支援も必要になる。そのため、医療の提供と介護の提供が同時に行われるので、在宅医療の内訳は「医療を提供する在宅医療」と「生活支援をする在宅介護」の2つのサービスがある。

　薬剤師が在宅医療にかかわる場合は、主治医の判断と患者の同意が必要である。薬剤師は患者の処方せんに基づいて調剤をするが、その時に患者が服薬し易いように工夫する。また、指示通りに服薬できているのかを確認して、薬の効果や副作用をモニターしている。このような薬物治療の適正化を確認する上から患者の自宅を訪問して、患者の療養状況、つまり、睡眠、食事、排泄などの他、家族や他職種からの情報を収集して、これらのモニター結果を主治医と共有して、薬物治療の適正化に貢献している。

　薬剤師の訪問活動は日本独自のものであり、近年、特にアジア隣国の注目を集めている。アジア在宅医療サミットも夢ではない。

串田一樹

Age-Related Macular Degeneration before and after the Era of Anti-VEGF Drugs

UNIT 14

加齢黄斑変性の治療が新たな時代を迎えている。本ユニットでは、加齢黄斑変性の薬物治療に関する研究を報じた記事を読む。記事の中では、2008年に始まった2年間の治験と、この治験の参加者を対象として治験終了後の2014年から2015年にかけて行われた5年後転帰の追跡調査という2つの研究が扱われているので、混同しないように注意しよう。

READING

2-11

age-related macular degeneration (AMD)
加齢黄斑変性
VEGF 血管内皮増殖因子
(vascular endothelial growth factor)
retina 網膜
light-sensitive
光感受性の

Age-related macular degeneration (AMD) is the leading cause of vision loss among older Americans. It causes damage to the central part of the retina, the light-sensitive tissue at the back of the eye. AMD often has very few symptoms in its early stages; but in later stages, it causes loss of the central, straight-ahead vision needed for activities like reading and driving.

geographic atrophy AMD 地図状萎縮加齢黄斑変性 (萎縮型加齢黄斑変性 [dry AMD] とも呼ばれる)
neovascular AMD
新生血管加齢黄斑変性
wet AMD
滲出型加齢黄斑変性

There are two types of late AMD—geographic atrophy AMD, and the more common neovascular AMD, also known as wet AMD. In neovascular AMD, fragile blood vessels grow under the retina and leak fluid. This usually starts in one eye, and is stimulated by a protein called VEGF. Just 10 years ago, people diagnosed with neovascular AMD were almost certain to develop severe vision loss in their affected eye and likely to lose vision in their other eye, too.

20/40 vision 20/40の視力 (欧米では視力を分数方式で表示する。日本の小数方式に相当するので、20/40は0.5に相当)

A new study looked at people with AMD who had regular treatment with drugs designed to block VEGF. After five years, 50 percent of them had 20/40 vision or better, 20 percent had

20/200 vision or worse, and the rest were in-between.

The Comparison of AMD Treatments Trials (CATT) began in 2008 and was designed to compare the anti-VEGF drugs Avastin and Lucentis. VEGF is important in the growth and development of new blood vessels. Avastin (bevacizumab) was approved by the Food and Drug Administration in 2004. Other drugs were later developed, with Lucentis (ranibizumab) coming to the market in 2006 and Eylea (aflibercept) in 2011. For treating AMD, the drugs are injected into the eye.

In the trial, more than 1200 participants with neovascular AMD were randomly assigned to receive either Lucentis or Avastin for two years, through monthly or as-needed injections. During that time, the two drugs were equally effective at preserving visual acuity.

The current study followed up with CATT participants between March 2014 and 2015, an average of 5.5 years after enrollment in the trial. After two years on their assigned drug, participants were free to work with their eye care providers to choose their own course of therapy. During that 3.5-year period, more than half received at least one treatment with a drug or therapy other than the drug assigned to them. The investigators obtained visual acuity measurements for 647 of 914 participants who were still living.

In addition to the overall effects of anti-VEGF therapy at five years, the investigators compared the outcomes of participants who received Avastin or Lucentis during the trial.

"At five years, there were no differences in visual acuity between the two drugs," said Daniel F. Martin, M.D., CATT study chair.

The study also found that after five years, participants assigned to Lucentis during the trial had a higher rate of strokes and heart attacks (7.6 percent) than those assigned to Avastin (4.5 percent). Since most participants received ⁵⁰ treatments other than their assigned drug after the two-year trial, the investigators are cautious about attributing this difference to the study drugs.

prognosis　予後
（疾患やけがの回復に関する
見通し）

ongoing　継続中の

"Although anti-VEGF treatment has greatly improved the prognosis for patients overall, we still need to find ways to ⁵⁵ avoid poor vision in these patients and to decrease the burden of ongoing treatment," said Maureen G. Maguire, Ph.D., the study's principal investigator.

National Eye Institute, "Age-related macular degeneration before and after the era of anti-VEGF drugs," press release (https://nei.nih.gov/news/pressrelease/AMD_before_after_anti-vegf_drugs)

14.1 COMPREHENSION QUESTIONS

Choose the best answer for each question based on the passage.

1. Which statement is true of neovascular AMD?

    (A) Blood vessels at the back of the eye are blocked, causing vision loss.

    (B) Neovascular AMD is more common than geographic atrophy AMD.

    (C) Both eyes are usually affected when the disease starts.

    (D) The production of VEGF is stimulated.

2. What was the objective of the CATT study?

    (A) To prevent the growth and development of new blood vessels

    (B) To determine the most effective dosage for Lucentis and Avastin

    (C) To compare two anti-VEGF drugs

    (D) To obtain FDA approval for a new drug

3. What did most of the CATT participants do after the trial was over?

    (A) They received one or more treatments that they had not received during the trial.

    (B) They continued to receive the same drug as in the trial.

    (C) They were continuously followed up with over the next few years.

    (D) They reviewed their treatment and its effects.

Unit 14　Age-Related Macular Degeneration before and after the Era of Anti-VEGF Drugs

4. Why do the investigators hesitate to conclude that Lucentis caused more side effects than Avastin?

(A) They still need to find ways to avoid poor vision in neovascular AMD patients.

(B) They do not want to offend the manufacturer of Lucentis.

(C) The difference was not significant.

(D) Factors other than the drugs may have affected the results.

14.2 PHARMACEUTICAL TERMINOLOGY

さまざまな医薬品 (1)

　ここで取り上げた医薬品は、いずれもよく使われるものばかりである。anthelminticは最近の日本ではあまり使用されないかもしれないが、発展途上国など海外で仕事をする場合には必須用語であろう。

● 練習問題

Match each of the following words with its definition below and then translate the word into Japanese.

1. antacid　　　（　　）　_____

2. anthelmintic　（　　）　_____

3. antidote　　　（　　）　_____

4. enema　　　　（　　）　_____

5. laxative　　　（　　）　_____

(a) a medicine or other remedy for counteracting the effects of poison

(b) a medicine used to destroy parasitic worms, also called vermifuge

(c) a procedure in which liquid or gas is injected into the rectum to expel its contents

(d) a substance that loosens stools and increases bowel movements, also called purgative

(e) a substance that neutralizes stomach acidity, used to relieve heartburn, indigestion or an upset stomach

14.3 GRAMMAR 「強調表現」

　　ある語句を強調するための表現法を強調表現という。文構造上、文頭に置くことにより語句は強調されるが、it is A that Bといった定番の表現を用いたり、否定語や感嘆表現を用いたりして、文意を強調することができる。

● 練習問題

次の各文の下線部に注意し、全文を日本語に訳しなさい。

1.　Although FDA has oversight of the dietary supplement industry, it is the supplement manufacturers and distributors that are responsible for making sure their products are safe before they're marketed.

　　_____

　　_____

2.　Endangered species are those that are in danger of being completely wiped out.

　　_____

　　_____

3.　Born on July 5th 1996, Dolly the sheep was the first mammal to be cloned from an adult cell.

　　_____

　　_____

4.　Not only did Darwin develop the idea of natural selection, he also presented compelling evidence from his detailed research which included a five-year voyage on the HMS* Beagle.　　*His [Her] Majesty's Shipの略。[女王]陛下の船の意味。

　　_____

　　_____

5.　What a proud thing for England if she is the first European nation which utterly abolishes slavery.

　　_____

　　_____

96

Unit 14 Age-Related Macular Degeneration before and after the Era of Anti-VEGF Drugs

14.4 LISTENING & SPEAKING

Listen to the following conversation and fill in the blanks based on the Japanese.

At a pharmacy.

Pharmacist: Good morning, may I help you?

Patient: Oh, hi! Yeah, I am looking for the pharmacy.

Pharmacist: You found the right person. 1. _____
_____.
(私と一緒にいらしてください。ご案内します)

Patient: Are you a pharmacist?

Pharmacist: Yes, I am. My name is Naoko Suzuki. Nice to meet you.

Patient: Hello Naoko. My name is Mohammed. I am so happy you can speak English.

Pharmacist: Not at all. 2. _____?
(日本へはご旅行ですか、それとも住んでいらっしゃるのですか)

Patient: I'm visiting for work. But 3. _____
_____.
(具合が悪くなって、初めて一人で病院に来ました)

Pharmacist: Here we are. 4. _____?
(処方箋を拝見してよろしいですか)

Patient: There you go. This is a very nice pharmacy. And it is quite big.

Pharmacist: Thanks. And yes, we are a new hospital and rather big as we take care of many patients and fill many prescriptions every day. I will now fill yours. Please have a seat.

Patient: Thank you so much. I'm so tired recently.

Pharmacist: Oh, I'm very sorry to hear that. But 5. _____
_____.
(このお薬を飲めばすぐによくなると思います)

Patient: I sincerely hope so.

14.5 WRITING

次の日本語を英語に訳しなさい。

1. 局所的に投与されたアトロピンは散瞳、つまり瞳孔の拡大を引き起こす。

   ヒント 局所的に投与された：topically applied

   アトロピン：atropine　散瞳：mydriasis　拡大する：dilate

   _____

   _____

2. チトクロームP450は、薬物代謝において酸化酵素として作用する。

   ヒント チトクローム：cytochrome　酸化酵素：oxidase

   _____

   _____

専門職連携教育（IPE）について思うこと

　専門職連携教育（IPE：Interprofessional Education）とは、他の職種の役割や専門性、また自身の職種の専門性や責任を理解するための教育のことである。英国のCAIPE（Centre for the Advancement of Interprofessional Education）は、IPEを「複数の領域の専門職者が連携およびケアの質を改善するために、同じ場所でともに学び、お互いから学びあいながら、お互いのことを学ぶこと」と定義している。チーム医療とは、「医療に従事する多種多様な医療スタッフが、各々の高い専門性を前提に、目的と情報を共有し、業務を分担しつつも互いに連携・補完し合い、患者の状況に的確に対応した医療を提供すること」である。このチーム医療の推進には、職種間の相互理解としてIPEが必要なものと考えられる。

　IPEが行われると、即戦力のあるチーム医療を実施出来る。そして最適な医療サービスが行われると、健康アウトカムの改善につながる。

　私は、大学生時代にIPEを受けておらず、多職種と接するのは卒業後であった。医療の課題を多職種と共有して、問題を解決していくプロセスはとても楽しいものである。

　学生のうちに、IPEを通じて多職種を理解し、コミュニケーション能力を高め、専門職連携による職務遂行方法を修得し、将来チーム医療において薬剤師の職能を発揮出来るように、頑張ろう。

小武家優子

Antibiotic / Antimicrobial Resistance

UNIT 15

ペニシリンが発見されてから、感染症の治療に大きな貢献をしてきた抗菌薬（抗生物質）であるが、その頻用、乱用により、細菌の「耐性化」が増え、効くはずの薬剤が効かない薬剤耐性菌感染症が世界中で脅威となっている。どのようにしてこの耐性と闘っていくか。その発生メカニズムと最新の取り組みを見てみよう。

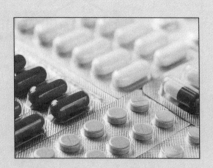

READING

 2-13

Antibiotics and similar drugs, together called antimicrobial agents, have been used for the last 70 years to treat patients who have infectious diseases. Since the 1940s, these drugs have greatly reduced illness and death from infectious diseases.
5   However, these drugs have been used so widely and for so long that the infectious organisms the antibiotics are designed to kill have adapted to them, making the drugs less effective. Each year in the United States, at least 2 million people become infected with bacteria that are resistant to antibiotics and at
10 least 23,000 people die each year as a direct result of these infections.

Antibiotic / Antimicrobial resistance is the ability of microbes to resist the effects of drugs—that is, the germs are not killed, and their growth is not stopped. Although some
15 people are at greater risk than others, no one can completely avoid the risk of antibiotic-resistant infections. Infections with resistant organisms are difficult to treat, requiring costly and sometimes toxic alternatives.

antimicrobial agent
抗菌薬(剤)

antibiotic-resistant infection
薬剤耐性菌感染症
toxic alternative
毒性のある別の治療法

99

How Resistance Happens and Spreads

The use of antibiotics is the single most important factor leading to antibiotic resistance around the world. Simply using antibiotics creates resistance. These drugs should only be used to manage infections.

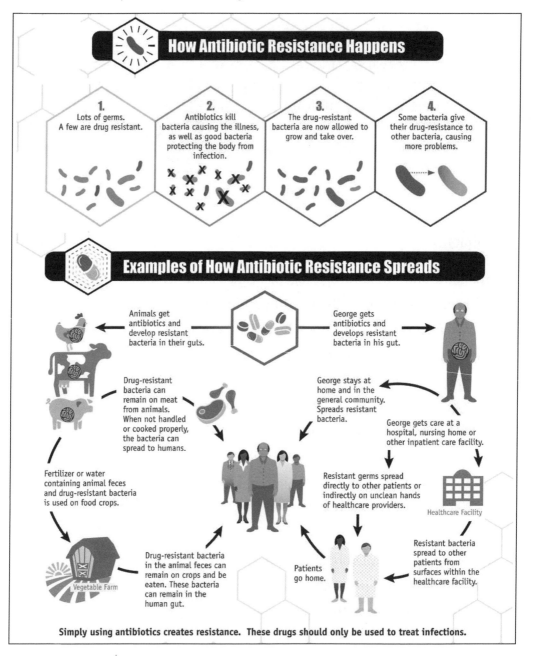

gut 消化管
contaminate 汚染する

The germs that contaminate food can become resistant because of the use of antibiotics in people and in food animals.

Unit 15 Antibiotic / Antimicrobial Resistance

For some germs, like the bacteria *Salmonella* and *Campylobacter*, it is primarily the use of antibiotics in food animals that increases resistance. Because of the link between antibiotic use in food-producing animals and the occurrence of antibiotic-resistant infections in humans, antibiotics that are medically important to treating infections in humans should be used in food-producing animals only under veterinary oversight and only to manage and treat infectious disease, not to promote growth.

The other major factor in the growth of antibiotic resistance is spread of the resistant strains of bacteria from person to person, or from the non-human sources in the environment.

Four Core Actions to Fight Resistance

1. PREVENTING INFECTIONS, PREVENTING THE SPREAD OF RESISTANCE

Avoiding infections in the first place reduces the amount of antibiotics that have to be used and reduces the likelihood that resistance will develop during therapy. There are many ways that drug-resistant infections can be prevented: immunization, safe food preparation, handwashing, and using antibiotics as directed and only when necessary. In addition, preventing infections also prevents the spread of resistant bacteria.

2. TRACKING

CDC gathers data on antibiotic-resistant infections, causes of infections and whether there are particular reasons (risk factors) that caused some people to get a resistant infection. With that information, experts can develop specific strategies to prevent those infections and prevent the resistant bacteria from spreading.

Salmonella サルモネラ菌
Campylobacter カンピロバクター菌

veterinary 獣医の

resistant strain 耐性株

CDC 疾病予防管理センター（Centers for Disease Control and Prevention）

101

antibiotic stewardship
抗菌薬適正使用支援（耐性菌
発現への対策として、抗菌薬
の適正使用を推進する取り組
み）

3. IMPROVING
ANTIBIOTIC PRESCRIBING/STEWARDSHIP

Perhaps the single most important action needed to greatly slow down the development and spread of antibiotic-resistant infections is to change the way antibiotics are used. Up to half of antibiotic use in humans and much of antibiotic use in animals is unnecessary and inappropriate and makes everyone less safe. Stopping even some of the inappropriate and unnecessary use of antibiotics in people and animals would help greatly in slowing down the spread of resistant bacteria. This commitment to always use antibiotics appropriately and safely—only when they are needed to treat disease, and to choose the right antibiotics and to administer them in the right way in every case—is known as antibiotic stewardship.

4. DEVELOPING NEW DRUGS AND DIAGNOSTIC TESTS

Because antibiotic resistance occurs as part of a natural process in which bacteria evolve, it can be slowed but not stopped. Therefore, we will always need new antibiotics to keep up with resistant bacteria as well as new diagnostic tests to track the development of resistance.

Centers for Disease Control and Prevention (CDC), About Antimicrobial Resistance (https://www.cdc.gov/drugresistance/about.html)

Unit 15 Antibiotic / Antimicrobial Resistance

⑮.1 COMPREHENSION QUESTIONS

Based on the passage, circle either T (true) or F (false) for each of the following statements.

1. Infectious bacteria can adapt to antibiotics and develop resistance.　　(T / F)

2. There is currently no treatment for drug-resistant bacteria.　　(T / F)

3. Antibiotic stewardship is a program that honors healthcare experts
   who prescribe antibiotics appropriately.　　(T / F)

Answer the following question in English.

How can drug-resistant bacteria spread to humans when antibiotics are used in animals? Briefly describe the process in two parts.

_____

_____

_____

⑮.2 PHARMACEUTICAL TERMINOLOGY

さまざまな医薬品 (2)

　ここで取り上げた医薬品は、いずれも接頭辞や接尾辞に注目すると自ずと意味が分かるものばかりである。

● 練習問題

Match each of the following words with its definition below and then translate the word into Japanese.

1. cardiotonic　(　)　_____
2. diuretic　　(　)　_____
3. hemostatic　(　)　_____

4. hypotensive　(　)　_____
5. thrombolytic　(　)　_____

(a) a substance that causes a blood clot to break up
(b) a substance that has a favorable effect upon the action of the heart
(c) a substance that lowers the blood pressure
(d) a substance that makes the body increase its production of waste fluids, causing increased passing of urine
(e) a substance that stops bleeding or hemorrhage

103

15.3 GRAMMAR 「分詞構文」

分詞構文は、2つの文を繋ぐのに接続詞の代わりに分詞を用いた構文をいう。接続詞＋S+V = Vingが基本形であり、便利な言い方である。

練習問題

次の各文の下線部に注意し、全文を日本語に訳しなさい。

1. <u>If left undiagnosed or untreated</u>, diabetes can lead to heart disease, stroke, kidney disease, blindness, and other health problems.

   _____

   _____

2. <u>Sometimes called the body's "master cells,"</u> stem cells are the cells that develop into blood, brain, bones, and all of the body's organs.

   _____

   _____

3. Grapefruit juice can block the action of these enzymes, <u>increasing the amount of drug in the body and may cause more side effects</u>.

   _____

   _____

4. <u>Covering a broad range of scientific fields such as biology, physics, astronomy and chemistry</u>, these men and women have pushed the world of science forward.

   _____

   _____

5. If you drink a lot of grapefruit juice while taking certain statin drugs to lower cholesterol, too much of the drug may stay in your body, <u>increasing your risk for liver and muscle damage that can lead to kidney failure</u>.

   _____

   _____

   _____

104

Unit 15   Antibiotic / Antimicrobial Resistance

15.4 LISTENING & SPEAKING

 2-14

Listen to the following conversation and fill in the blanks based on the Japanese.

At a pharmacy.

Pharmacist: Mr. Mohammed Azir?

Patient: Yes, that's me.

Pharmacist: I have filled your prescription. You have three medications today. Is that right?

Patient: Yes. 1. _____
_____.
（医師の先生は、そのうちの2つが胃のためで、3つめが抗生物質だとおっしゃっていました）

Pharmacist: This is correct. Now I will explain how to take them. 2. _____
_____.
（この1つめのお薬はカプセル剤で、朝食を召し上がったあとで一日1個飲みます）
Please be sure to take it with a tall glass of water. There are seven capsules in total.

Patient: I understand. How about that medicine?

Pharmacist: Your next medicine is in powder form. You should be careful when opening it. After opening it, 3. _____.
（必ず中身をすべて口の中に入れてください）
Once in your mouth, be sure to drink lots of water to help you swallow it. Take this after each meal for one week.

Patient: Will it taste bad?

Pharmacist: I'm afraid so. In Japan, 4. _____
_____.
（私たちは良薬は口に苦しと考えるのを好みます）

Patient: We have a similar saying in my country, too.

Pharmacist: The third medicine is in tablet form. Take two of them twice a day after breakfast and dinner. This prescription is for one week, too.

Patient: I understand. Thank you so much!

Pharmacist: You are very welcome. 5. _____
_____. Please take care!
（ご不明な点があれば、ご遠慮なくこの電話番号にお電話ください）

105

15.5 WRITING

次の日本語を英語に訳しなさい。

1. アセチルコリン受容体遮断薬は、アセチルコリンがその受容体に結合するのを妨げ、受容体を不活性状態に保つ。

   ヒント アセチルコリン受容体遮断薬：acetylcholine receptor blocker

2. ベンゾジアゼピン系薬剤は、一般的に使用されている鎮静催眠薬であり、抗けいれん作用もある。

   ヒント ベンゾジアゼピン系薬剤：benzodiazepines　鎮静催眠薬：sedative-hypnotic
   anticonvulsant：抗けいれんの

機械化による薬剤師業務の変革

　近年、保険薬局の業務は「対物」から「対人」へとシフトしている。2015年10月に「患者のための薬局ビジョン」が策定され、かかりつけ薬局機能を中心に健康サポート機能や高度薬学管理機能をもった薬局が求められている。現在までの調剤業務はほとんど人の手によるものであった。そこで、処方入力から薬剤ピッキング、散薬調剤を機械化し調剤業務を効率化することで対人業務の充実を目指している。

　処方箋に載っている二次元バーコードを読み込むと、全自動PTPシート払い出し装置（ロボピック®）、散剤調剤ロボット（ディメロ®）、ピッキングサポートシステム（ポリムス®）がそれぞれ連動し、調剤作業を行う。可能な限り機械化することで、薬剤の規格・剤形間違いや単純な取り違えはなくなり正確性・安全性がさらに増した。また機械による調剤作業の記録が残ることで、薬の過不足を訴える患者のなかに、認知機能低下が疑われる症例を発見し、在宅医療につながる症例も増えてきている。どこよりも早く機械を導入することで、我々もシステム開発に関わり、現場の意見が強く反映された調剤機器を導入している。

　日常業務の負担軽減が薬剤師を本来の業務へ導き、ハイリスク薬の丁寧な服薬指導、在宅医療の推進、専門資格の取得、地域包括ケアシステムなど、地域のかかりつけ機能を発揮することが可能になった。

高橋　恵・高橋俊明

Academic Research in the 21st Century

UNIT 16

研究論文の捏造、研究費の不正使用などの問題が後を絶たない今日、研究倫理に関する事前研修が義務付けられ、倫理審査委員会で研究の妥当性が容認されなければ研究に着手することはできない。四半世紀前には考えられなかった状況である。では、なぜそのような厳格なプロセスが必要なのか、どのような要因があるのか、米国での現状を読んで、研究倫理について考えてみよう。

READING

 2-15

　　The incentives and reward structure of academia have undergone a dramatic change in the last half century. Competition has increased for tenure-track positions, and most U.S. PhD graduates are selecting careers in industry,
5 government, or elsewhere partly because the current supply of PhDs far exceeds available academic positions. Universities are also increasingly "balancing their budgets on the backs of adjuncts" given that part-time or adjunct professor jobs make up 76% of the academic labor force, while getting paid on
10 average $2,700 per class, without benefits or job security. There are other concerns about the culture of modern academia, as reflected by studies showing that the attractiveness of academic research careers decreases over the course of students' PhD program relative to other careers, reflecting the overemphasis
15 on quantitative metrics, competition for limited funding, and difficulties pursuing science as a public good.

incentive 報酬・利益による動機（cf. motivation 人が持っているやる気）
academia （大学などの）学術研究的環境、学術界
tenure-track 終身在職権のある

adjunct 非常勤教職員

Quantitative performance metrics: effect on individual researchers and productivity

The goal of measuring scientific productivity has given rise to quantitative performance metrics, including publication count, citations, combined citation-publication counts (e.g., h-index), journal impact factors (JIF), total research dollars, and total patents. These quantitative metrics now dominate decision-making in faculty hiring, promotion and tenure, awards, and funding. Because these measures are subject to manipulation, they are doomed to become misleading and even counterproductive, according to *Goodhart's Law*, which states that *"when a measure becomes a target, it ceases to be a good measure"*.

Ultimately, the well-intentioned use of quantitative metrics may create inequities and outcomes worse than the systems they replaced. Specifically, if rewards are disproportionally given to individuals manipulating their metrics, problems of the old subjective paradigms (e.g., old-boys' networks) may be tame by comparison. In a 2010 survey, 71% of respondents stated that they feared colleagues can "game" or "cheat" their way into better evaluations at their institutions, demonstrating that scientists are acutely attuned to the possibility of abuses in the current system.

It is instructive to conceptualize the basic problem from a perspective of emphasizing quality-in-research versus quantity-in-research, as well as effects of perverse incentives. Assuming that the goal of the scientific enterprise is to maximize true scientific progress, a process that overemphasizes quality might require triple or quadruple blinded studies, mandatory replication of results by independent parties, and peer-review of all data and statistics before publication—such a system would minimize mistakes, but would produce very few results due to overcaution. At the

Unit 16 Academic Research in the 21st Century

50 other extreme, an overemphasis on quantity is also problematic because accepting less scientific rigor in statistics, replication, and quality controls or a less rigorous review process would produce a very high number of articles, but after considering costly setbacks associated with a high error rate, true progress
55 would also be low. A hypothetical optimum productivity lies somewhere in between, and it is possible that our current practices (enforced by peer review) evolved to be near the optimum in an environment with fewer perverse incentives.

replication　追試（実験）

What Kind of Profession Are We Creating for the Next
60 *Generation of Academics?*

So I have just one wish for you—the good luck to be somewhere where you are free to maintain the kind of integrity I have described, and where you do not feel forced by a need to maintain your position in the organization, or financial support, or so on, to lose your
65 *integrity. May you have that freedom*—Richard Feynman, Nobel laureate

Marc A. Edwards and Siddhartha Roy, "Academic Research in the 21st Century: Maintaining Scientific Integrity in a Climate of Perverse Incentives and Hypercompetition." *Environmental Engineering Science.* Volume 34, Number 1, 2017

Mary Ann Liebert, Inc. DOI: 10.1089/ees.2016.0223

16.1 COMPREHENSION QUESTIONS

Answer the following questions in English.

1. Why are most U.S. PhD graduates choosing careers other than academic positions?

   _____

2. Why do the U.S. PhD students lose their interest in academic research while they are in the program?

   _____

   _____

109

3. How does the U.S. academia evaluate individual researchers and productivity?

   _____

4. What is a weak point of quantitative metrics?

   _____

5. What does the author think about the ideal evaluation?

   _____

16.2 PHARMACEUTICAL TERMINOLOGY

さまざまな医薬品 (3)

　ここで取り上げた医薬品名のうち、gargleは擬音語からできた語である。医学英語には、belchまたはburb（げっぷ）、murmur（心雑音）、wheeze（喘鳴）など症状を表すもので擬音語からできたものがいくつかある。

● 練習問題

Match each of the following words with its definition below and then translate the word into Japanese.

1. expectorant （　　） _____

2. gargle （　　） _____

3. narcotic （　　） _____

4. sedative （　　） _____

5. anesthetic （　　） _____

(a) an addictive drug affecting mood or behavior

(b) a liquid held in the throat and kept in motion by a stream of air from the lungs to wash or rinse the throat or mouth

(c) a medicine that helps loosen mucus so you can cough it up

(d) a medicine that promotes calm or induces sleep

(e) a substance that induces insensitivity to pain

Unit 16 Academic Research in the 21st Century

16.3 GRAMMAR 「省略」

　省略は、前後関係から文意を容易に理解できる時に文の一部を省略する表現法であり、簡潔な英語にするための方法である。

練習問題

次の各文のうち、省略できる語（句）を略し、簡潔な文にしなさい。

1. The two enantiomers can be difficult to distinguish; one form smells of lemons but the other form smells of oranges.

   _____

   _____

2. Dark surfaces such as black paper absorb more light and heat than lighter ones such as white paper do.

   _____

   _____

3. She told Jimmy to come at ten and Bob to come at eleven.

   _____

   _____

4. It is better to be late in doing it than never to do it.

   _____

   _____

5. Being surrounded by the sea, the country has a mild climate.

   _____

   _____

111

16.4 LISTENING & SPEAKING

 2-16

Listen to the following conversation and fill in the blanks based on the Japanese.

At a pharmacy.

Patient: Excuse me, 1. _____.
(私の薬のことで助けていただきたいのですが)

Pharmacist: Yes, how may I help you?

Patient: I came here yesterday and got three medicines. I took two of them and I had no issues. But 2. _____
_____.
(この粉末剤を飲んだら、ひどい胃痛になったのです)

Pharmacist: Oh, I am so sorry to hear that. May I see your package?

Patient: Here you go.

Pharmacist: OK, let me call your doctor about this prescription and see 3. _____
_____. Please have a seat.
(ほかに使えるお薬があるかどうか)

Patient: Thank you so much. I was so surprised because I never had a problem taking a medicine before.

Pharmacist: I see. Let me call her and see what she says.

(Pharmacist makes a phone call.)

Pharmacist: She has written a new prescription for you. 4. _____
_____.
(それは別のお薬ですが、胃の助けにもなります)

Patient: Oh, I am so happy to hear that! Thank you so much for all of your help.

112

Unit 16　Academic Research in the 21st Century

16.5 WRITING

次の日本語を英語に訳しなさい。

1. 降圧療法は、脳卒中や心筋梗塞といった高血圧の合併症を予防することを目指す。

    ヒント 降圧療法：antihypertensive therapy

    _____

    _____

2. 降圧薬の1グループである利尿薬は、主に体内からナトリウムを除去し血液量を減らすことによって血圧を下げる。

    ヒント 血液量：blood volume

    _____

    _____

医師国家試験には英語の問題がある!?

　社会の国際化に伴い、医師が臨床や研究の場で医学英語を使用する機会は確実に増加している。2009年実施の医師国家試験から医学英語問題が問われるようになり、設問も進化し続けている。導入当初3年間は症候の英語表記を選ばせるような語彙問題だった。例えば2012年には次のような医学英語語彙問題が出題された。

> 設問：症候と英語表記の組合せで誤っているのはどれか。
> 選択肢：　a 黄 疸　jaundice　　　b けいれん convulsion　　　c 不整脈 anorexia
> 　　　　　d 脱 水　dehydration　　e 便 秘　　constipation

　2015年からは100語足らずの英文症例報告や紹介状が出題されるようになった。英文症例報告を読み、その診断名の英語表記を問うなどの問題である。例えば2018年には次のような問題が出題された。

> A 78-year-old female passenger has developed swelling of her left lower leg towards the end of a long-haul flight. She does not complain of any pain at rest. She has pitting edema of her left lower leg but no color or temperature changes are observed. Calf pain is induced on dorsiflexion of her left foot. Because she suffers from shortness of breath, the possibility of pulmonary embolism should be considered, and transfer to an appropriate hospital is advised.
> 設問：原因として考えられるのはどれか。
> 選択肢：　a Acute kidney injury　　b Deep venous thrombosis　　c Femoral neck fracture
> 　　　　　d Heart failure　　　　　e Peripheral disease

　医学英語問題が医師国家試験の全問題中に占める割合は2%足らずであるが、以前は皆無だったことを考えると大きな変化である。医師の医学英語力向上の重要性が改めて認識されている表れであろう。

玉巻欣子

Appendix

Appendix

文法一覧表

1. 5文型

第1文型 (S + V)　　　　LDL stands for low-density lipoprotein.
　　　　　　　　　　　　LDLとは、低密度リポタンパク質を表す。

第2文型 (S + V + C)　　Leprosy is an infectious disease. (S = C)
　　　　　　　　　　　　ハンセン病は感染症である。

第3文型 (S + V + O)　　Lead can affect many different parts of the body. (S ≠ O)
　　　　　　　　　　　　鉛はさまざまな身体部位に影響する可能性がある。

第4文型 (S+V+IO+DO)　They will give you further instructions. (IO ≠ DO)
　　　　　　　　　　　　彼らはあなたにさらなる指示を与えるだろう。

第5文型 (S + V + O + C)　Some foods can make the problem worse. (O = C)
　　　　　　　　　　　　一部の食品は問題を悪化させる可能性がある。

2. 名　詞

種類： 普通名詞、物質名詞、抽象名詞、固有名詞、集合名詞、
　　　 名詞相当語句（動名詞、不定詞、that-節など）

働き： 文の主語　　　　*Vitamins* are important for our health.
　　　　　　　　　　　　ビタミンはわれわれの健康にとって重要である。

　　　 動詞の補語　　　A virus is an invisible *microorganism*.
　　　　　　　　　　　　ウイルスとは、目に見えない微生物である。

　　　 動詞の目的語　　Watson and Crick discovered the *structure* of DNA.
　　　　　　　　　　　　ワトソンとクリックはDNAの構造を発見した。

　　　 前置詞の目的語　Patients with *cancer* need a special treatment.
　　　　　　　　　　　　がん患者は特別な治療を必要とする。

3. 形容詞

働き： 限定用法 = 名詞を修飾する

　　　 前位の形容　　　E. Coli is a *typical* bacterium.
　　　　　　　　　　　　大腸菌は典型的な細菌である。

　　　 後位の形容　　　Diabetes is a strong risk factor *for heart* disease.
　　　　　　　　　　　　糖尿病は心臓病の強力な危険因子である。

　　　 叙述用法 = 補語になる

　　　　　　　　　　　　Malnutrition is very *harmful* to your health.
　　　　　　　　　　　　栄養不良は健康にとって非常に有害である。

4. 副　詞

種類： 副詞、疑問副詞、関係副詞句、副詞相当語句（分詞、不定詞、前置詞句）

働き： 形容詞を修飾　　Eat foods that are *naturally* low in fat.
　　　　　　　　　　　もともと脂肪分の少ない食品を食べなさい。

　　　　副詞を修飾　　He speaks English *very* well.
　　　　　　　　　　　彼は英語をとても上手に話す。

　　　　動詞を修飾　　Cholesterol builds up *inside your blood vessels*.
　　　　　　　　　　　コレステロールは血管の内部に蓄積する。

　　　　文全体を修飾　*In general*, those over age 50 need higher amounts of vitamin D.
　　　　　　　　　　　一般的に、50歳を超えた人は、より大量のビタミンDを必要とする。

意味： 時、条件、目的、原因、理由、結果、譲歩、付帯状況、様態、程度、頻度などを表す。

5. 代名詞

種類： 人称代名詞(he、she、I)、指示代名詞(this、that)、不定代名詞(someone、anybody)、疑問代名詞(who、what)、関係代名詞(which、whose、that、what)

働き： 名詞と同じ

6. 動名詞

名詞的用法のみ

　　　　文の主語　　　*Freezing* food slows or stops bacteria's growth.
　　　　　　　　　　　食品の冷凍は、細菌の増殖を遅延または阻止する。

　　　　動詞の目的語　Finish *eating* at least 2 hours before you go to bed.
　　　　　　　　　　　少なくとも就寝の2時間前には食べるのを終えなさい。

　　　　補語　　　　　Good treatments are *helping* patients live longer.
　　　　　　　　　　　すぐれた治療とは、患者がより長生きするのを助けることである。

　　　　前置詞の目的語 After *eating* foods with lactose in them, you may feel sick.
　　　　　　　　　　　ラクトースを含有する食品を食べたあと、あなたは具合が悪くなるかもしれない。

Appendix

7. 不定詞

種類： to + 動詞の原形、動詞の原形のみ

働き： 名詞的用法　The role of insulin is *to move glucose from the bloodstream into muscle, fat, and liver cells*, where it can be used as fuel.
インスリンの役割は、グルコースを燃料として利用できる筋肉、脂肪、肝細胞の中へ、血流中から移行させることである。

形容詞的用法　Medication *to treat diabetes* is called insulin.
糖尿病を治療するための薬はインスリンと呼ばれる。

副詞的用法　*To insert an aspirin suppository into the rectum*, follow these steps.
アスピリン坐剤を直腸に挿入するには、以下の手順に従うこと。

8. 分　詞

種類： 現在分詞、過去分詞

働き： 形容詞の限定用法　Foodborne illnesses are caused by eating food *contaminated with bacteria, parasites, or viruses*.
食品媒介性疾患は、細菌、寄生虫、またはウイルスに汚染された食品を食べることによって生じる。

形容詞の叙述用法　Their lungs become *congested* with mucus and are likely to get respiratory infections.
彼らの肺は粘液がたまり、呼吸器感染症にかかりやすくなる。

副詞的用法　Brain tumors are classified *depending* on the exact site of the tumor.
脳腫瘍は腫瘍の正確な部位によって分類される。

9. 接続詞

種類： 等位接続詞＝左右同等のものを結ぶand、but、or、nor、for（というのは）

従属接続詞＝主部と述部からなる文を導いて名詞節、副詞節を作る
that、whether、if（～かどうか）、when、while、as、after、before、because、as、since、though、although、evenif、even though、if、 suppose、unlessなど

119

10. 前置詞

働き：名詞・代名詞の前に置かれ、前置詞句を形成する

形容詞的用法　Patients *with malignant tumors* need special care.
悪性腫瘍の患者には、特別なケアが必要である。

副詞的用法　*Despite its name*, the H1N1 flu can't be caught by eating pork products or being near pigs.
その名にかかわらず、H1N1インフルエンザはブタ肉製品を食べたりブタのそばへ行ったりしても感染しない。

11. 文の種類

単文　主部と述部からなる文が一つ
Acidic water is dangerous to plants.
酸性の水は植物にとって危険である。

重文　等位接続詞が文と文を左右につないだもの
Daily physiotherapy helps to relieve congestion, and antibiotics are used to fight infections.
毎日の理学療法は鬱滞の解消を助け、感染症と戦うために抗生物質が使われる。

複文　従属接続詞＋S＋V～, S＋V～. または S＋V～, 従属接続詞＋S＋V～.

混合文　従属接続詞＋S＋V～ and (but, or) S＋V～, S＋V～.

12. 仮定法

働き： 仮定の条件や願望などを表す

種類： 仮定法現在　<u>It's very important</u> that antiviral drugs *be used* early to treat flu in people who are very sick.
非常に具合の悪い人のインフルエンザを治療するには、抗ウイルス薬を早期に使用することがきわめて重要である。

CDC <u>recommends</u> that you *stay* home for at least 24 hours after your fever is gone.
CDCは発熱がおさまってから少なくとも24時間は外出しないことを推奨している。

仮定法過去　If ＋ S ＋ (助)動詞の過去形…, S ＋ would (should, could, might)＋原形

仮定法過去完了　If ＋ S ＋ 動詞の過去完了形…, S ＋ would (should, could, might)＋完了形

Word Parts in Medical Terminology

　英語の医学用語はギリシャ語もしくはラテン語に基づいており、複雑に見えるが一定の形式を持っているので、世界に共通する言語である。ほとんどの医学用語は、構成要素(word part)である語根(root)、接頭辞(prefix)、接尾辞(suffix)に分けることができる。これらのワードパートはどのように使われても同じ意味を持つので、ワードパートを学ぶことで多くの医学用語を理解することができる。

　語根(root)は、各医学用語の中心的単位であり、その語の基本的意味を担っている。しかしほとんどの語根は単独では完全な用語にはならない。接頭辞(prefix)は語根の前に付く短い部分、接尾辞(suffix)は語根の後に付く短い部分であり、これらが語根に意味を加えて一つの用語を作っている。

　複雑な用語は語根を二つ以上含んでいる。語根と語根を連結するとき、また子音で始まる接尾辞が語根に付くとき、発音を容易にするために母音（通常o）が挿入される。これを連結母音と呼び、語根と連結母音がくっついたものを連結形という。

　語根は分野によって異なる意味を持つことがあり、発音や意味によって上記のルールに例外も生ずるが、それらはワードパートを学ぶことで自ずと理解できるようになるであろう。

word part	meaning	example
a-	not, without, lack of, absence	atom（原子）
ab-	away from	abnormal（異常の）
ad-	toward, near	adhere（付着する）
aden/o	gland	adenitis（腺炎）
adip/o	fat	adipoid（脂肪様の）
adren/o, adrenal/o	adrenal gland, epinephrine	adrenopathy（副腎疾患）
aer/o	air, gas	aerobic（好気性の）
-al	pertaining to	vocal（声の）
-algia	pain	gastralgia（胃痛）
an-	not, without, lack of	anarithmia（失算症）
angi/o	vessel	angioblastoma（血管芽細胞腫）
ante-	before	antecedent（前駆体）
anti-	against	antiagglutinin（抗凝集素）
arter/o, arteri/o	artery	arteriogram（動脈造影）
arthr/o	joint	arthralgia（関節痛）
-ase	enzyme	protease（蛋白質分解酵素）
audi/o	hearing	audiovisual（視聴覚の）
auto-	self	autoimmunity（自己免疫）
bacteri/o	bacterium	bacterial（細菌性の）
bi-	two, twice	bipolar（双極性の）
blast/o	immature cell, productive cell, embryonic cell	blastoma（芽細胞腫）

word part	meaning	example
brachi/o	arm	brachial (上腕の)
brady-	slow	bradycardia (徐脈)
bronch/i, bronch/o	bronchus	bronchiectasis (気管支拡張)
bucc/o	cheek	intrabuccal (頬内の)
carcin/o	cancer, carcinoma	carcinogen (発癌物質)
cardi/o	heart	cardiology (心臓学)
cephal/o	head	microcephaly (小頭症)
cerebell/o	cerebellum	intracerebellar (小脳内の)
cerebr/o	cerebrum	decerebrate (除脳する)
chem/o	chemical	chemotherapy (化学療法)
chol/e, chol/o	bile, gall	cholecyst (胆嚢)
chrom/o, chromat/o	color, stain	chromoprotein (色素蛋白)
chron/o	time	chronometry (時間測定法)
circum-	around	circumference (周縁)
col/o, colon/o	colon	colocystoplasty (結腸膀胱形成術)
contra-	against	contraceptive (避妊薬)
crani/o	skull, cranium	craniocerebral (頭蓋脳の)
cyan/o-	blue	cyanosis (チアノーゼ)
-cyte, cyt/o	cell	cytology (細胞学)
de-	down, without, removal, loss	debilitant (弱める)
dent/o, dent/i	tooth	dentist (歯科医)
derm/o, dermat/o	skin	dermatologist (皮膚科医)
dextr/o-	right	dextrality (右利き)
di-	two, twice	disaccharide (二糖類)
dia-	through	diameter (直径)
dipl/o	double	diplococcal (双球菌の)
dis-	absence, removal, separation	disinfection (消毒)
duoden/o	duodenum	duodenitis (十二指腸炎)
dys-	abnormal, painful, difficult	dyspnea (呼吸困難)
ec-	out, outside	eccentric (偏心性の)
ecto-	out, outside	ectopia (偏位)
-ectomy	excision, surgical removal	nephrectomy (腎摘出)
electr/o	electricity	electrocardiogram (心電図)
embry/o	embryo	embryology (発生学)
-emia	condition of blood	anemia (貧血)
encephal/o	brain	encephalopathy (脳症)
end/o-	in, within	endoscope (内視鏡)

Appendix

word part	meaning	example
endocrin/o	endocrine	endocrinology (内分泌学)
enter/o	intestine	enteritis (腸炎)
epi-	upon, over	epidermal (表皮の)
erythr/o-	red, red blood cell	erythrocyte (赤血球)
esophag/o	esophagus	esophageal (食道の)
eu-	true, good, easy, normal	euthanasia (安楽死)
ex/o	away from, outside	exocrine (外分泌の)
extra-	outside	extracellular (細胞外の)
fet/o	fetus	fetoglobulins (胎児蛋白)
fibr/o	fiber	fibroblast (繊維芽細胞)
-form	like, resembling	epileptiform (てんかん様の)
galact/o	milk	galactometer (乳脂計)
gangli/o, ganglion/o	ganglion	gangliocyte (神経節細胞)
gastr/o	stomach	gastroenteritis (胃腸炎)
gen/o, -gen, -genesis	origin, formation	genetics (遺伝学)
gluc/o	glucose	glucogenic (糖生成の)
glyc/o	sugar, glucose	glycogen (糖質)
-gram	record of data	echogram (超音波像)
-graph	instrument for recording data	polygraph (ポリグラフ)
-graphy	act of recording data	radiography (X線撮影法)
hem/o, hemat/o	blood	hemorrhage (出血)
hemi-	half, one side	hemisphere (脳半球)
-hemia	condition of blood	erythrocythemia (赤血球増加症)
hepat/o	liver	hepatoma (肝癌)
hetero-	other, different, unequal	heterosexual (異性愛の)
hist/o, histi/o	tissue	histology (組織学)
homo-, homeo-	same, unchanging	homogeneous (均質の)
hydr/o	water, fluid	hydrate (水和物)
hyper-	over, excess, increased, abnormally high	hypertension (高血圧)
hypn/o	sleep	hypnogenic (催眠の)
hypo-	under, below, decreased, abnormally low	hypotension (低血圧)
hyster/o	uterus	hysteromyomectomy (子宮筋腫切除)
-ia	condition of	anaesthesia (知覚麻痺)
-ian	specialist	physician (医師、内科医)
-iatrics	medical specialty	pediatrics (小児科学)
-iatry	medical specialty	psychiatry (精神医学)
-ic	pertaining to	allergic (アレルギーの)

123

word part	meaning	example
-ical	pertaining to	physical (身体的な)
im-	not	imbalance (不均等)
immun/o	immunity, immune system	immunology (免疫学)
in-	not	inactivate (不活性化する)
infra-	below	infracardiac (心臓直下の)
inter-	between	interosseous (骨間の)
intra-	in, within	intravenous (静脈内の)
-ism	condition of	alcoholism (アルコール症)
iso-	equal, same	isotope (同位体)
-ist	specialist	cardiologist (心臓病専門医)
-itis	inflammation	gastritis (胃炎)
juxta-	near, beside	juxtaposition (近位)
kine, kinesi/o, kinet/o	movement	pharmacokinetics (薬物動態学)
lact/o	milk	lactose (乳糖)
laryng/o	larynx	laryngoscope (喉頭鏡)
-lepsy	seizure	narcolepsy (睡眠発作)
leuk/o-	white, colorless, white blood cell	leukocyte (白血球)
-lexia	reading	dyslexia (難読症)
lingu/o	tongue	sublingual (舌下の)
lip/o	fat, lipid	lipocyte (脂肪細胞)
-logy	study of	physiology (生理学)
lymph/o	lymph, lymphatic system, lymphocyte	lymphoid (リンパ球様の)
macro-	large, abnormally large	macrophage (大食細胞)
mal-	bad, poor	malnutrition (栄養失調)
mamm/o	breast, mammary gland	mammography (乳房レントゲン撮影法)
-mania	excited state, obsession	toxicomania (麻薬中毒)
mast/o	breast, mammary gland	mastadenitis (乳腺炎)
medull/o	inner part, medulla oblongata	medulloblastoma (髄芽細胞腫)
mega-, megalo-	large, abnormally large	megacolon (巨大結腸)
melan/o	black, dark, melanin	melanoma (黒色腫)
men/o, mens	month, menstruation	menstrual (月経の)
-meter	instrument for measuring	thermometer (体温計)
micro-	small, one millionth	microorganism (微生物)
-mimetic	mimicking, simulating	cholinomimetic (コリンに似た作用の)
mon/o	one	monoclonal (単一クローンの)
morph/o	form, structure	morphogenetic (形態発生の)
multi-	many	multivalent (多価性の)
muscul/o	muscle	musculoskeletal (筋骨格の)

Appendix

word part	meaning	example
myel/o	bone marrow, spinal cord	myeloblast (骨髄芽細胞)
narc/o	stupor, unconsciousness	narcoleptic (睡眠薬)
nas/o	nose	nasal (鼻の)
necrosis	death of tissue	osteoradionecrosis (骨放射線壊死)
neo-	new	neoblastic (新生組織の)
nephr/o	kidney	nephritis (腎炎)
neur/o, neur/i	nervous system, nerve	neuropathy (神経障害)
normo-	normal	normovolemia (正常血液量)
nucle/o	neucleus	nucleolus (核小体)
ocul/o	eye	oculomotor (眼球運動の)
-oma	tumor	carcinoma (癌腫)
onc/o	tumor	oncology (腫瘍学)
ophthalm/o	eye	ophthalmologist (眼科医)
opt/o	eye, vision	optic (眼の)
ortho-	straight, correct, upright	orthosis (装具)
-ose	sugar	fructose (果糖)
-osis	condition of	tuberculosis (結核)
oste/o	bone	osteoporosis (骨粗しょう症)
ot/o	ear	otalgia (耳痛)
pancreat/o	pancreas	pancreatitis (膵臓炎)
para-	near, beside	paracentral (中心近くの)
path/o, -pathy	disease	pathophysiology (病態生理学)
-penia	decrease in, deficiency of	leukopenia (白血球減少症)
per-	through	percutaneous (経皮の)
peri-	around	peripheral (末梢の)
phag/o	eat, ingest	phagocyte (食細胞の)
pharmac/o	drug	pharmacology (薬理学)
-phasia	speech	heterophasia (錯語症)
phleb/o	vein	phlebography (静脈造影)
phobia	fear	hydrophobia (恐水病)
phon/o	sound, voice	phonocardiogram (心音図)
phot/o	light	photosensitive (日光過敏)
plas, -plasia	formation, molding, development	neoplasia (腫瘍形成)
-pnea	breathing	dyspnea (呼吸困難)
pneum/o, pneumat/o	air, gas, lung respiration	pneumonia (肺炎)
pneumon/o	lung	pneumonococcus (肺炎球菌)
poly-	many, much	polyarthritis (多発性関節炎)

word part	meaning	example
post-	after, behind	postnasal (後鼻腔の)
pre-	before, in front of	premature (未熟の)
prim/i-	first	primary (最初の、原発 (性)の)
pro-	before, in front of	proactivator (前駆賦活体)
pseudo-	fasle	pseudoanemia (偽性貧血)
psych/o	mind	psychology (心理学)
pulm/o, pulmon/o	lung	pulmonary (肺の)
quadr/i-	four	quadribasic (四塩基の)
radi/o	radiation, X-ray	radiotherapy (放射線治療)
re-	again, back	recurrence (再発)
rect/o	rectum	rectoabdominal (直腸腹部の)
ren/o	kidney	renogenic (腎原性の)
-rhage, rhagia	bursting forth, profuse flow, hemorrhage	hemorrhage (出血)
-rhea	flow, discharge	diarrhea (下痢)
rhin/o	nose	rhinitis (鼻炎)
sclerosis	hardening	arteriosclerosis (動脈硬化症)
-scope	instrument for viewing or examining	endoscope (内視鏡)
-scopy	examination of	laryngoscopy (喉頭鏡検査法)
semi-	half, partial	semicircular (半円の)
-sis	conditon of	nephrolithiasis (腎石症)
somat/o	body	somatogenic (体細胞原性の)
-some	small body	ribosome (リボソーム)
somn/i, somn/o	sleep	somniloquy (催眠談話)
spasm	sudden contraction, cramp	graphospasm (書痙)
splen/o	spleen	splenorrhagia (脾出血)
stasis	suppression, stoppage	homeostasis (恒常性)
sub-	below, under	subabdominal (腹部下方の)
super-	above, excess	superactivity (過度活動性)
syn-, sym-	together	synapse (接合部)
tachy-	rapid	tachypnea (頻呼吸)
therm/o	heat, temperature	thermometer (体温計)
thromb/o	blood clot	thrombocyte (血小板)
thym/o	thymus gland	thymocyte (胸腺細胞)
-tomy	incision of, cutting	anatomy (解剖学)
tox/o, toxic/o	poison, toxin	toxicology (毒物学)
trache/o	trachea	tracheal (気管の)
trans-	through, across, beyond	transaction (相互作用)

Appendix

word part	meaning	example
tri-	three	triacid (三酸塩基)
trop/o, -tropic	act(ing) on, affect(ing)	psychotropic (向精神性の)
un-	not	unsaturated (不飽和の)
uni-	one	unicellular (単細胞の)
-uria	urine, urination	hemoglobinuria (血色素尿症)
ur/o	urine, urinary tract	urology (泌尿科学)
urin/o	urine	urinate (排尿する)
uter/o	uterus	uterocervical (子宮頚部の)
vas/o	vessel, duct, vas deferens	vasoconstriction (血管狭窄)
vascul/o	vessel	vasculogenesis (脈管形成)
ven/o, ven/i	vein	venography (静脈造影法)
vertebr/o	vertebra, spinal column	vertebral (脊椎の)
xanth/o-	yellow	xanthoderma (皮膚黄変)
xero-	dry	xerosis (乾燥症、乾皮症)

PROFESSIONAL COMPETENCIES FOR PHARMACISTS

1. Professionalism: Fulfill the legal, ethical, and professional responsibilities of pharmacists.

2. Patient-oriented attitude: Respect the rights of individuals and promote the health and welfare of patients and consumers.

3. Communication skills: Communicate effectively with patients, consumers, and other healthcare professionals to provide necessary information.

4. Interprofessional team-care: Collaborate with healthcare teams in hospitals and regional communities.

5. Basic sciences: Understand the effects of medicines and chemicals on living bodies and the environments.

6. Medication therapy management: Contribute to the optimal use of medicines through pharmaceutical care.

7. Community health and medical care: Contribute to public health and pharmaceutical hygiene and enhance community healthcare and home care.

8. Research: Engage in research on drug development and the appropriate use of medicines to improve the healthcare environment.

9. Lifelong learning: Continue lifelong professional development in response to the advances in healthcare.

10. Education and training: Contribute to the development of the next generation of professional pharmacists.

To ensure that pharmacists acquire professional competencies, general instructional objectives (GIOs) and specific behavioral objectives (SBOs) were established.

"PROFESSIONAL COMPETENCIES FOR PHARMACISTS"

Model Core Curriculum for Pharmacy Education (2013 Version) p.3

https://www.pharm.or.jp/kyoiku/pdf/corecurri_eng180426.pdf

薬剤師として求められる基本的な資質

豊かな人間性と医療人としての高い使命感を有し、生命の尊さを深く認識し、生涯にわたって薬の専門家としての責任を持ち、人の命と健康な生活を守ることを通して社会に貢献する。
6年卒業時に必要とされている資質は以下のとおりである。

（薬剤師としての心構え） 医療の担い手として、豊かな人間性と、生命の尊厳についての深い認識をもち、薬剤師の義務及び法令を遵守するとともに、人の命と健康な生活を守る使命感、責任感及び倫理観を有する。

（患者・生活者本位の視点） 患者の人権を尊重し、患者及びその家族の秘密を守り、常に患者・生活者の立場に立って、これらの人々の安全と利益を最優先する。

（コミュニケーション能力） 患者・生活者、他職種から情報を適切に収集し、これらの人々に有益な情報を提供するためのコミュニケーション能力を有する。

（チーム医療への参画） 医療機関や地域における医療チームに積極的に参画し、相互の尊重のもとに薬剤師に求められる行動を適切にとる。

（基礎的な科学力） 生体及び環境に対する医薬品・化学物質等の影響を理解するために必要な科学に関する基本的知識・技能・態度を有する。

（薬物療法における実践的能力） 薬物療法を主体的に計画、実施、評価し、安全で有効な医薬品の使用を推進するために、医薬品を供給し、調剤、服薬指導、処方設計の提案等の薬学的管理を実践する能力を有する。

（地域の保健・医療における実践的能力） 地域の保健、医療、福祉、介護及び行政等に参画・連携して、地域における人々の健康増進、公衆衛生の向上に貢献する能力を有する。

（研究能力） 薬学・医療の進歩と改善に資するために、研究を遂行する意欲と問題発見・解決能力を有する。

（自己研鑽） 薬学・医療の進歩に対応するために、医療と医薬品を巡る社会的動向を把握し、生涯にわたり自己研鑽を続ける意欲と態度を有する。

（教育能力） 次世代を担う人材を育成する意欲と態度を有する。

出典：薬学教育モデル・コアカリキュラム 平成25年度改訂版
「薬剤師として求められる基本的な資質」 pp.16-17
http://www.mext.go.jp/component/a_menu/education/detail/__icsFiles/afieldfile/2015/02/12/1355030_01.pdf

執筆者一覧

*編集委員　**副責任者　***責任者

* Reading, Comprehension Questions

Unit 1	竹内典子	明治薬科大学（前）
Unit 2	堀内正子***	昭和薬科大学　英語研究室
Unit 3	堀内正子	
Unit 4	齋藤弘明	日本大学薬学部　有機化学研究室
Unit 5	板垣　正	日本大学薬学部　病原微生物学研究室
	河野享子	京都薬科大学　学生実習支援センター
Unit 6	高橋和子	神奈川県立保健福祉大学　人間総合科
Unit 7	平井清子	北里大学一般教育部　基礎教育センター　英語
Unit 8	吉澤（渡邉）小百合	星薬科大学　教育学研究室
Unit 9	井原久美子	昭和薬科大学（英語非常勤）
Unit 10	高橋和子	
Unit 11	竹内典子	
Unit 12	田沢恭子**	明治薬科大学（英語非常勤）
Unit 13	玉巻欣子*	神戸薬科大学　英語第二研究室
Unit 14	田沢恭子	
Unit 15	井原久美子	
Unit 16	金子利雄*	日本大学薬学部　英語1研究室

* Pharmaceutical Terminology (Units 1~16)

玉巻欣子

* Grammar (Units 1~16)

金子利雄

* Writing (Units 1~16)

高橋和子

* Listening & Speaking (Units 1~16)

エリック・スカイヤー*　日本大学薬学部　英語2研究室
井原久美子、高橋和子、堀内正子

＊ 文法一覧表（Appendix）

金子利雄

＊ Word Parts in Medical Terminology (Appendix)

竹内典子

＊ コラム

Unit 1	沖﨑　歩	国立がん研究センター東病院　緩和医療科
Unit 2	大山　龍	アーティスト・薬剤師
Unit 3	川名三知代	薬局薬剤師
Unit 4	齋藤弘明	
Unit 5	赤瀬智子	横浜市立大学　大学院医学研究科・医学部　看護生命科学／周麻酔期看護学
Unit 6	堀内正子	
Unit 7	萩原裕美	薬局ホームケアファーマシー田無店
Unit 8	小泉龍士	国立研究開発法人　国立国際医療研究センター　病院薬剤部薬剤師レジデント
Unit 9	千代田尚己	ジョンソン・エンド・ジョンソン株式会社　メディカルカンパニー
Unit 10	高橋香織	製薬メーカー勤務
Unit 11	岩澤真紀子	北里大学薬学部　臨床薬学研究・教育センター臨床薬学　（医薬品情報学）
Unit 12	門谷靖裕	医療法人　沖縄徳洲会　湘南鎌倉総合病院　薬剤部
Unit 13	串田一樹	昭和薬科大学　寄付講座　地域連携薬局イノベーション
Unit 14	小武家優子	第一薬科大学　地域医療薬学センター
Unit 15	高橋　恵	トモエ薬局
	高橋俊明	
Unit 16	玉巻欣子	

TEXT PRODUCTION STAFF

edited by Masato Kogame	編集 小亀 正人
English-language editing by Bill Benfield	英文校閲 ビル・ベンフィールド
cover design by Ruben Frosali	表紙デザイン ルーベン・フロサリ
text design by Ruben Frosali	本文デザイン ルーベン・フロサリ

CD PRODUCTION STAFF

recorded by	吹き込み者
Howard Colefield (AmerE)	ハワード・コールフィールド（アメリカ英語）
Rachel Walzer (AmerE)	レイチェル・ウォルツァー（アメリカ英語）
Josh Keller (AmerE)	ジョシュ・ケラー（アメリカ英語）
Emma Howard (BritE)	エマ・ハワード（イギリス英語）

English for Student Pharmacists 2
薬学生のための英語 2

2019年1月20日　初版 発行
2023年3月 5 日　第5刷 発行

著　者　日本薬学英語研究会（JAPE）
発行者　佐野 英一郎
発行所　株式会社 成美堂
　　　　〒101-0052　東京都千代田区神田小川町3-22
　　　　TEL 03-3291-2261　FAX 03-3293-5490
　　　　https://www.seibido.co.jp

印刷・製本　（株）加藤文明社

ISBN 978-4-7919-7194-7　　　　　　　　　　Printed in Japan

・落丁・乱丁本はお取り替えします。
・本書の無断複写は、著作権上の例外を除き著作権侵害となります。